The Power of the
20s

Pip Dunn

An imprint of
Ian Allan Publishing

Frontispiece:
A cement train from Earles Sidings rounds the curve on the Dore-avoiding line as it heads towards Chesterfield with a train for Beeston in 1989, with Trainload Coal Nos 20 140 and 20 154 in charge. This was not a booked duty for '20s' — a Class 37 would have been more common. *Peter Rose*

Title page:
The third of the class delivered, No D8002, spent several years in London before moving to Toton in August 1969. It was dual-braked in 1970 and in May 1974 moved to Scotland where it spent the next 12 years at Eastfield depot. On 6 June 1978 it ambles past Newton-on-Ayr with an empty coal train heading for one of the numerous Ayrshire pits. It still has oval buffers, which it retained until withdrawn in 1988. *Norman Preedy*

First published 2007

ISBN (10) 0 86093 611 2
ISBN (13) 978 0 86093 611 4

© Ian Allan Publishing Ltd 2007

Published by Oxford Publishing Co

an imprint of Ian Allan Publishing Ltd, Hersham, Surrey, KT12 4RG

Printed in England by Ian Allan Publishing Ltd, Hersham, Surrey, KT12 4RG

Code: 0711/B

Visit the Ian Allan Publishing website at www.ianallanpublishing.com

Contents

Foreword

Neil McNicholas, Managing Director,
Direct Rail Services

It is fair to say DRS owes a sizeable chunk of its success to the Class 20. We started operations in 1996 with a fleet of just five overhauled '20s' and slowly expanded the fleet to 15 before acquiring other locomotive types — and, indeed, another six '20s'.

Never racehorses, '20s' have proved supremely rugged and reliable in hauling nuclear flask traffic across the UK. In more recent times they proved ideal for railhead treatment trains — running top-and-tail across Yorkshire and East Anglia.

DRS now runs an expanding and profitable business, with brand-new Class 66s on 75mph intermodal trains. This owes much to the success of the early DRS operations just over a decade ago — and much of that is down to the versatility of the '20s'.

Of course, any business needs good staff, and our drivers like the '20s', while their uncomplicated design means fitters find them easy to work on, allowing reduced downtime and thus enabling them to return to traffic after maintenance with relative ease.

Our 10th-anniversary staff train in August 2006 showed how dependable the type is. When a Class 37 failed we had a single Class 20 hauling 500 tonnes up the stiff gradient to Ais Gill in driving rain, which it did commendably. We were even on time at Leeds! Such performances give credibility to the belief among the old BR staff that Class 20s 'will always get you home'.

DRS is an expanding company, but we see no reason to eliminate the Class 20s just yet; they are tailor-made for much of our work, and we envisage using them for many years to come. They may be elderly, but that is not a problem. They are a credit to English Electric and its staff.

Neil McNicholas
Carlisle
October 2007

Below:
Those on board an attractive narrowboat glance over at the railway when they hear the noise of Nos 20 310/311 hard at work on a RHTT crossing the River Ouse at Ely in November 2005. *Peter Foster*

Introduction

The Class 20s have achieved an impressive five decades of service on Britain's railways by virtue of their simplicity, dependability, reliability and versatility. Among rail enthusiasts they never gained a huge following, as they lacked the glamour, speed and names of the big passenger engines. They spent 99% of their lives hauling freight trains and were usually dirty as a result. But they rarely let you down.

In the early 1980s, when my interest in railways started, most of my friends liked the big passenger locomotives — the 'Peaks', '50s', 'Deltics' and so on. Others liked the all-rounders, the '37s', '40s' and '47s' especially. But on 14 January 1984 I experienced something that I will never forget, and which made me realise the Class 20s were the machines for me. On a Leamington Spa–Edinburgh day excursion we were stopped at Abingdon, 15 miles south of Carstairs, as heavy snow had brought the overhead wires down; so Nos 20 114 and 20 002 hauled us to Carstairs. But the return journey was even better, as No 20 083 hauled our dead electric and heavy train, on its own, back from Carstairs to Abingdon. I will never forget the sight and sound of this 1,000hp machine, with sparks flying from its exhaust ports in the freezing, dark night air with a brilliant white blanket all around it. From that day I decided I would channel my efforts into supporting these wonderful machines. My application to join the fledgling Class 20 Locomotive Society was in the post a few days afterwards!

Only a few books have been written about Class 20s, but since *Profile of the Class 20s* (OPC, 1983, out of print), only *Class 20s in Colour* (Fell, Midland Publishing, 1994, out of print) and *Class 20 Photofile* (Dunn & Loader, Vanguard Publishing, 2005) have hit the shelves. I hope, therefore, that *The Power of the 20s* will go some way to addressing that shortfall in commemorating these wonderful locomotives in their 50th-anniversary year.

I have deliberately tried to avoid using too many previously published pictures, although it is inevitable that some have been seen before. There is also far more to Class 20s than hauling coal trains in Nottinghamshire and Scotland, and I have tried to illustrate that.

Of course, covering 50 years in just 280-odd pictures is always going to be difficult, and it is inevitable some small piece of the class's history may have been overlooked.

Of the 228 Class 20s built between 1957 and 1968 a handful survive working, and the type still has a future on the main line, both with Direct Rail Services and Harry Needle Railroad Company. The latter also has placed some machines with industrial users; 2006 saw locomotives overhauled for use with Corus, and more could follow.

Several '20s' — nicknamed 'Choppers', 'Mooses' or 'Bombs' by enthusiasts — are preserved at heritage railways up and down the country, allowing them to be enjoyed by the public as well as providing a useful role for hauling maintenance trains and the like.

In its 50 years the class has travelled virtually every line in the country as well as seeing use further afield: four were used in France for a decade from 1992, and the type has even worked in Kosovo. The Class 20s have paid for themselves several times over, and at a time when the railway favours the new-build General Motors Class 66 it is satisfying to see one of the UK's finest-ever locomotive designs still at work. Long may it continue.

Pip Dunn
Peterborough,
October 2007

Below:
On 26 July 1977 Tinsley-based Nos 20 214 and 20 215 pass the closed station at Shirebrook hauling a vacuum-braked freight. On the left is a line of new Class 56s just entering traffic which, along with new air-braked MGR hoppers, would displace Class 20s on to other work. *John Chalcraft*

Right:
In the early 1970s Toton depot staff would chalk the locomotive's running number on the top of the buffer-beam. Because it has recently been renumbered under the TOPS system, No 20 067 still has 8067 chalked on the front as it arrives at Gloucester with No 20 148 on 14 June 1974 with a Bescot—Severn Tunnel Junction freight, a train '20s' would often work throughout. No 20 067 also retains its steampipe hose.
Norman Preedy

Right:
Already 33 years old, Pilot Scheme No 20 013 and No 20 075 stand inside Toton TMD on 22 April 1990. No 20 013 was withdrawn on 13 December the following year, having amassed 34 years and one month in traffic, although it did have several periods in store.
J. Porter / Ivan Stewart collection

Left:
A modeller's dream, Dr Beeching's nightmare! No D8082 shunts wagons at Falkland Yard that will form an unfitted mixed freight for Polmadie in October 1961. At this time diesels were still 'new fangled' machinery and many failures were simply down to the crews' unfamiliarity with the new kit. Once they had settled in, Class 20s soon became the most reliable of all early diesel types, regularly achieving over 90% availability — a figure only surpassed when the Class 66s arrived at the turn of the century. *Bill Hamilton*

Early days in traffic

Right:
With its shunting complete, No D8082 sets off for Polmadie with a long mixed freight mainly comprising mineral wagons with coal for Glasgow and the surrounding areas. *Bill Hamilton*

Left:
Concerned over the visibility of diesels to track workers, British Railways started applying yellow panels to the fronts of locomotives. Widespread introduction of BR blue from 1965 saw full yellow ends adopted and these were also applied to green locomotives pending their call to works when they would be painted blue. On 7 April 1969 No D8019 shows this livery variation at its then home depot, Stratford. *John Chalcraft*

Above:
Two filthy green Class 20s, led by No D8120, pass Uddingston Junction in the Glasgow suburbs in January 1964 with a Ravenscraig–General Terminus train of empty ore wagons. At this time Class 17s were entering traffic, but they were to prove less than successful so 100 further '20s' were soon ordered. *Author's collection*

Right:
In October 1961 No D8084 ambles between Prestwick and Falkland Yard in Ayrshire with a mixed freight, just a month into its career. This is one of the 15 Class 20s still in day-to-day use with DRS, now numbered 20 302 and in its 46th year of service which has taken it to all manner of locations — including France while used on Channel Tunnel tracklaying.
Bill Hamilton

Above:
This May 1960 picture shows No D8002 leading No D8009, another of the 20 Pilot Scheme machines, on a lengthy freight past Rugby. When new, the '20s' were in all-over Brunswick green with red buffer-beams and grey bonnet roofs. Half yellow panels were added from the early 1960s and then full yellow ends. The first '20s' in BR blue were those built from No D8180 onwards in 1966 while repaints of green locomotives also started in the same year. *Danny Preston*

Left:
Just three months old, last-built No D8327 stands at its then home depot of Polmadie on 12 May 1968. In front is No D8095 showing the common livery at the time for Scottish blue '20s' — no wrap-round yellow ends on the nose end. No D8327 would not change much for 17 years, other than being renumbered 20 227 in December 1973, but was repainted in Railfreight livery in 1985 and withdrawn on 1 October 1990, only to be sold for preservation a year later. *David Percival*

Right:
No D8049, complete with bodyside ladder, stands in the goods yard at Royston with a pick-up freight in 1964. Class 20s were based at Great Northern depots at Hornsey and later, from 1959, Finsbury Park, but the last were moved away in April 1966. *Peter Ingarfill*

Right:
Built for freight, Class 20s were not fitted with steam-heat boilers, but in the summer they did find passenger work from early on in their careers. On 1 August 1960 No D8027, no doubt substituting for an unavailable 'Baby Deltic', passes Hadley Wood with a commuter train from King's Cross. *John Chalcraft*

Left:
On 19 June 1960 Class V2 2-6-2 No 60874 failed at Knebworth on the 09.10 Cleethorpes–King's Cross, so No D8046 was summoned from Hitchin to take over. With the correct headcode displayed, the trusty Type 1 waits for its 25 miles of express-passenger work. *David Percival*

Left:
The Leicester–Burton line, via Coalville, was a busy freight route with numerous branches serving quarries, collieries and power stations. Today it is much reduced in importance, but back in the 1970s it was a real hotspot for freight, with many of the trains worked by '20s'. On 17 July 1974 No 20 198 leads No 20 081 into the sidings at Coalville Mantle Lane. At this time many photographers ignored '20s', preferring to chase the last Class 52 'Westerns'.
Phil Hawkins

In the 1970s

Below:
Recently renumbered from No D8194 and No D8042, Toton's Nos 20 194 and 20 042 head north from the yards adjacent to their home depot on 17 July 1974. The train is typical for this era, a rake of loaded 16-tonne coal wagons. Renumbering into the TOPS system was slow; the first '20s' changed were Nos 20 032/185 in September 1973, the last a year later, with the majority in February/March of 1974. *Phil Hawkins*

Above:
Nos 20 181 and 20 192 haul a northbound mixed freight through Loughborough on 10 July 1975 while 31 316 shunts ballast wagons in the sidings. All locomotives have four-character headcodes, although displaying the appropriate reporting number was no longer required, hence the Class 20s' incomplete headcode. *Phil Hawkins*

Centre right:
A pair of dual-braked '20s', Nos 20 155 and 20 154, pass Coalville Mantle Lane signalbox on 10 July 1975 with a ballast train. At this time many '20s' were still in BR green livery — usually in very shabby condition and with TOPS numbers often crudely applied. The last '20' painted blue was No 20 141 in 1980, while No 20 014 was withdrawn in green — the only '20' not painted blue. *Phil Hawkins*

Right:
Passing the packed marshalling yard at Washwood Heath, Birmingham, are Toton's Nos 20 081 and 20 157 heading under the M6 motorway at Bromford Bridge with a southbound freight on 9 October 1975. *Phil Hawkins*

Left:
With just one of its black-rimmed discs displayed, No 20 043 leads No 20 070 over the level crossing at Coalville on 17 July 1974 with a loaded coal train. At this time there were still nine operational rail-served pits on the Leicester–Burton line alone. *Phil Hawkins*

Right:
Another typically busy freight yard from 1975 as Nos 20 032 and 20 022 leave Tinsley on 24 July. No 20 032 does not have a cabside number, as in the early 1970s several '20s' were released with numbers on the bodyside just in front of the cab — not the best place to put them for photographers, spotters or depot staff alike! Other examples to have numbers on the bodyside include Nos 8076/100/102/112/117 and 20 058/081. *Phil Hawkins*

Right:
With a long train of vacuum-braked hoppers, Tinsley's Nos 20 206 and 20 214 pass Wath on 24 July 1975. At this time Tinsley had a sizeable allocation of Class 20s, which worked alongside '25s', '31s', '37s' and '40s' on freight throughout Yorkshire. *Phil Hawkins*

Right:
Class 20s were never allocated to Western Region depots, apart from Eastfield's Nos 20 179/201 being sent to Cardiff Canton in May 1979 for two weeks' 'loan' for evaluation prior to possible use in the area, a trial never pursued. In BR ownership, an occasional flirtation with the area was some pairs' running to Didcot Power Station with coal trains, but even these were relatively rare. On 16 September 1979 Nos 20 159 and 20 071 pass Oxford with a northbound freight train. *Brian Daniels*

Above:
Two Pilot Scheme machines reunited as Tinsley's Nos 20 001 and 20 005 pass Melton Mowbray on 26 April 1983 with an eastbound mixed freight. By this time six of the original 20 machines had been withdrawn — leaving six in use at Tinsley, one at Toton and seven in Scotland — either in traffic or in store pending dual-braking. No 20 001 survives in preservation with the Class 20 Locomotive Society. *John Chalcraft*

A decade of change – the 1980s

Left:
Built in 1957 and withdrawn in 1988, No 20 002 spent its 31 years in BR service working from many depots. In the early 1980s it was a Scottish locomotive and on 22 June 1981 had a day as station pilot at Glasgow Queen Street, taking ECS into and out of the station. Sometimes '20s' would bank passenger trains up the stiff incline to Cowlairs. *John Chalcraft*

Right:
Class 20s were never all that common on oil trains in the Midlands, but on 10 August 1983 Nos 20 077 and 20 178 remove a rake of empty oil tankers from Willington Power Station, near Derby. *John Tuffs*

Above:
A wonderful southbound mixed freight on 29 October 1982 passes Hathern, near Loughborough, behind Toton's Nos 20 163 and 20 176. Both new to Toton on 23 September 1966 and 16 November 1966 respectively, No 20 163 spent its entire career allocated to the depot, yet was scrapped in Scotland at MC Metals in May 1994. No 20 176 had spells at Tinsley, Immingham and Thornaby, but it too was disposed of by the Glaswegian scrap merchant, in January 1994. *John Tuffs*

Left:
In the summer of 1983 five Scottish Class 20s, dual-braked, slow-speed control Nos 20 179/184/191/217/219 moved to Toton, which for the latter two was their first move south of the border since delivery in 1967. They were mainly used on merry-go-round coal trains, pending more of Toton's fleet being dual-braked. Nos 20 191 and 20 179 arrive at Willington Power Station from Denby opencast colliery on 10 August. In the background Nos 20 136/141 amble past with a mixed northbound freight, two vacuum-braked locomotives that spent their entire careers working from LMR depots. *John Tuffs*

Right:
Another duty the '20s' picked up as the rundown of the Class 25s gathered momentum was the sand trains to Oakamoor in the Potteries. On 27 August 1986 Nos 20 188 and 20 121 depart with train 9L37, the 15.35 empties to Longport, which will go forward the following day to Ravenhead Junction, St Helens. The PAA hoppers had just been introduced, replacing old vacuum-braked wagons. These trains lasted until 1989, but Class 20 action was to return to this line, as Nos D8007/154 were, until 2007, preserved on the route that reopened as the Churnet Valley line. *Paul Shannon*

Below right:
An unusual duty for Class 20s was on 23 August 1989 when Departmental-sector Nos 20 139 and 20 160 were hired by the Trainload Construction sector to fill in for a Leicester-outbased Class 56 to work a Redland self-discharge train, seen passing Toton Yard. Both spent the majority of their careers at Toton, although No 20 139 spent June 1982-March 1985 in Scotland, followed by two years at Tinsley and Immingham. It moved to France in 1992 when sold to CFD, while some 18 months after No 20 160 was withdrawn, it was painted by Bescot Depot with red cabs and 'named' *Bescot Bo-Bo* for a depot open day. *J. Porter /*

Above:
Tinsley's Nos 20 146 and 20 144 descend from the Wirksworth Incline to the yard adjacent to the closed station on 30 September 1985 with a stone train of HTV vacuum-braked hoppers. The wagons will be joined to those on the left and the train will head to Duffield to rejoin the main line to Derby for overnight stabling and then onward to King's Lynn.
John Tuffs

Right:
Another unusual working for a pair of Departmental-sector '20s' was on 23 August 1989 when Nos 20 199 and 20 202 hauled an empty Peak Forest-bound stone train, standing in for a pair of Buxton Class 37s. They approach Toton Yard where they will be replaced.
J. Porter / Ivan Stewart collection

BR's Speedlink wagonload network provided work for Class 20s until it was axed in July 1991 as uneconomic. Passing Toton Yard with a northbound working on 23 August 1989 are Immingham's Trainload Metals Nos 20 061 and 20 126. In the late 1980s Immingham depot started applying orange cantrail stripes to its fleet — as demonstrated by No 20 061, which is also missing two of its discs. *J. Porter / Ivan Stewart collection*

Before Class 20s became established on nuclear flask traffic with DRS, such workings in BR days were rare, especially onto the Western Region. However, as a foretaste of what was to come, and in a rare foray in the Western Region, Nos 20 055 and 20 151 whistle away from Westbury with a diverted train from Bridgwater on 8 May 1985. Today's trains no longer have to run with brake vans. *John Chalcraft*

On 25 October 1985 Tinsley's Nos 20 165 and 20 107 pull out of the loop at Melton Mowbray as they head west with a train of empty hoppers. After several years, with the fleet decimated by withdrawals and locomotives in store, BR had 210 Class 20s in traffic, the highest level since 1981. *John Chalcraft*

Wagonload freight

Left:
Nos 20 020 and 20 072 pass Peak Forest with 7F17, the 15.45 Peak Forest South–Walton Old Junction Speedlink wagonload freight on 9 September 1986. The leading locomotive has a Motherwell leaping salmon emblem on its nose-end bodyside door, a trend that started in the mid-1980s with Eastfield applying West Highland terriers to be followed by Haymarket with castles and then Motherwell's fish. Wigan Springs Branch, briefly, applied a pork pie motif to a few '20s', although probably more in jest than seriousness! No 20 020 is now preserved at Bo'ness while No 20 072 is in store with HNRC.
John Tuffs

Below:
Local trip freight work occupies Nos 20 211 and 20 185 at Charlestown Junction in Scotland on 22 March 1990 as they propel their train from Thornton Junction to the RNAD site at Crombie. No 20 211 has 'HST' stencilled on its buffer-beam above the drawhook, signifying it is capable of hauling an HST set if so required. *Steve Turner*

Right:
Class 20s still work acid trains today, using DRS '20/3s', but back in BR days a pair would often be provided for trips in the North West. Nos 20 013/057 pull out of the loop at St Helen's Central with the 11.05 Ravenhead Junction–Warrington Arpley, with two sulphuric acid tanks for onward shipment to Dalry in Ayrshire on 11 November 1991. *Paul Shannon*

Chemical Brothers

Below:
Eastfield's Nos 20 137 and 20 148 come off the Methil branch at Thornton with a short train of carbon dioxide tanks from Cameron Bridge. Two locomotives for such a featherweight load may seem like overkill, but to all intents and purposes a pair of '20s' were used as Type 4s and splitting them was not always practical. They also gave the added insurance, that if one failed, the other would get the train home, or at least clear of the running line. *Paul Shannon*

Above:
In 1989 three Eastfield Class 20s — Nos 20 066/148/185 — were allocated to the Trainload Petroleum sector to provide a pair to work out of Grangemouth. On 17 July Nos 20 185 and 20 148 approach Greenhill Lower Junction with a Prestwick–Grangemouth empty fuel oil train. No 20 185 is one of the several ex-Immingham '20s' with an orange cantrail stripe. *Max Fowler*

Below:
Class 20s were very rare on Cambrian lines until the late 1980s when, following driver training at Shrewsbury, along with Class 37s they replaced Class 25s on freight on the line to Aberystwyth. The once-a-week oil train from Stanlow was one duty that became an occasional Class 20 turn in 1987, and on 6 April 1988 Nos 20 040 and 20 170 have just arrived at the terminal with 6J28, the 01.00 from Stanlow. Class 37s took over this working shortly afterwards, and in April 1993 it ceased running. *Paul Shannon*

Left:
Framed nicely by the loaded
column, Nos 20 135 and 20 080
arrive at Silverdale colliery with
an empty MGR that, once loaded
with coal, will head to Fiddlers
Ferry Power Station on 3 May
1990. This picture encapsulates the
typical kind of work in that decade
to great effect. *Steve Turner*

Coal, coal and more coal

Right:
On 6 October 1976 Tinsley's
Nos 20 127 and 20 017 trundle past
the new-build houses at Kiveton
Park on the Worksop–Sheffield
line with a motley selection of
loaded coal wagons. The rear
locomotive was withdrawn in
1982, as BR decided four stored
'20s' should be sacrificed from
the dual-braking programme to
yield parts to others. These were
Nos 20 003/017/020/027, although
No 20 020 was later reinstated
when dual-braked No 20 036 had an
accident and was declared beyond
economic repair. No 20 017 was
scrapped in March 1985, but
No 20 127 is still in traffic today
as 20 303. *Tom Heavyside*

Above:
Beautifully framed by the signals, two Toton vacuum-braked machines are deep into Tinsley territory! No 20 172 leads No 20 193 past Treeton Junction, with its wonderful signalbox, on 30 June 1982 with an up coal train.
Peter Rose

Above:
The delightful Denby branch, near Derby, was regularly worked by Class 20s collecting coal from the colliery at the end of the 4½-mile line. On 23 August 1990 No 20 187 leads No 20 052 with a fully loaded train of HAA hoppers for Toton Yard for onward shipment to Didcot, probably behind a Class 58. *Steve Turner*

Above right:
On 14 September 1979 Nos 20 067 and 20 041 wait patiently at Drakelow East Curve Junction to head to Coalville Mantle Lane with an empty train of coal wagons, having just discharged at the nearby power station while another pair take a loaded coal train from Cadley Hill Colliery to Willington. *The late A. O. Wynn*

Below:
Class 20s were a familiar sight on Ayrshire coal trains from their introduction, although the wagons were progressively updated. On 13 July 1988 Nos 20 192 and 20 227 haul 32 MGR coal hoppers out of Ayr Harbour with the 09.48 empties to Knockshinnoch Colliery for reloading.
Paul Shannon

Left:
Two Toton veterans together: Nos 20 141/143 approach Moira West Junction on the Burton–Coalville line on 1 November 1979 with a rake of empty HTV coal hoppers returning from Drakelow Power Station. Both were scrapped at MC Metals in August 1993. *John Tuffs*

Left:
At Latchford Sidings, Warrington, on 3 May 1990 Nos 20 172 and 20 028 leave with a MGR coal train having run round while Nos 20 182 and 20 175 wait to follow. In 1986 Class 20s returned to the North East at Thornaby and some were spruced up with red solebars and unofficial names — Nos 20 028 *Bedale*, 20 070 *Leyburn*, 20 172 *Redmire* and 20 173 *Wensleydale* — to mark their use on limestone trains on the Northallerton–Redmire line.
In 1987 BR officially named the first Class 20s when Thornaby's Nos 20 118/122/137/165 were named *Saltburn- by-the-Sea*, *Cleveland Potash*, *Murray B. Hofmeyr* and *Henry Pease* respectively. *J. Porter / Ivan Stewart collection*

Left:
So filthy is No 20 089 that it is hard to distinguish its number as it leads No 20 137 through Prestwick on 2 June 1977 with a southbound coal train. As with many Scottish locomotives, the Region did not consider it worth the effort to remove snowploughs for the summer. *Brian Morrison*

Above:
In the spring of 1989 the WCML was closed for engineering work on several weekends, resulting in freight trains being diverted via Clapham, Hellifield and Clitheroe. Nos 20 028 and 20 172 come off the Carnforth line at Settle Junction hauling the heavy-loaded Mossend–Dee Marsh steel train on 11 March 1989. Both show evidence of their days at Thornaby — red solebars, kingfisher logos and, in the case of No 20 172, large bodyside numbers.
Paul Shannon

Right:
On July 28 1992, Nos 20 118 and 20 137 wander past the closed station building at Deepcar, northern Sheffield, taking scrap metal to Stocksbridge for reprocessing. They will continue into the loop, run round and then move to the headshunt to propel into the exchange sidings where a steelworks industrial shunter will collect the wagons. *Author*

Odd jobs

Above:
Class 20s were never common on the Manchester–Woodhead–Sheffield line before closure on 18 July 1981, but in the days soon after, several were used on recovery trains when the track was lifted. On 22 October 1983, over two years since the last electric trains ran, Tinsley's No 20 056 trundles eastwards with two well wagons at Dunford Bridge, one end of the famous 3-mile, 64yd tunnel. The wires are long gone, but the overhead stanchions remain. *Les Nixon*

Left:
On 2 June 1989 Nos 20 005 and 20 099 pilot Trainload Metals Class 37/5s Nos 37 520 and 37 507 *Hartlepool Pipe Mill* on a Corby–Lackenby steel train past Melton Mowbray. Presumably one of the '37s' had failed. *Barry Adams*

Right:
Showing the signs that it had not been overhauled for over seven years, tatty No 20 072 leads No 20 197 past Shipley Gate, north of Ilkeston in the Erewash Valley, with the 13.00 Melton Mowbray–Adwick (Manchester) intermodal freight conveying pet food. The date is 6 October 1987, by which time BR had ceased overhauls on '20s' and had started to run down the class; in November 13 were withdrawn in one go, some just 20 years old. *John Tuffs*

Below:
Toton's snowplough-fitted No 20 166 hauls Class 313 EMU No 313 029 past Barrow-on-Soar, between Loughborough and Trent Junction, on 8 March 1979 as it takes the unit north. As the EMU is air-braked only, and the '20' is vacuum-braked only, the train would be running as an unfitted freight. *John Chalcraft*

Left:
Not a Skegness train leaving Burton on 9 July 1985 but Nos 20 080 and 20 094 with a mixed rake of Mk 1, 2 and 3s including High Speed track-recording coach DB999950 as the second vehicle. At this time Toton depot was experimenting with 'permanently-coupled' pairs, which led to many '20s' staying together for several months — including this duo. The experiment was not pursued. *John Tuffs*

Above:
Although '20s' could often reach Severn Tunnel Junction, visits further west in South Wales were rare. On 31 March 1987 Nos 20 001/098 pass Newport station, with a Cardiff Canton–Derby Etches Park ECS, with Departmental coaches DB977330/339. Both '20s' are preserved, at Butterley and nearby Loughborough respectively. *John Tuffs*

West Highland wonders

Right:
No 20 138 is stabled on Fort William depot on 18 May 1988. In 1987 radio electronic token block signalling was introduced on the West Highland lines so Eastfield fitted three '20s' with the necessary RETB equipment — with nose-mounted aerials. No 20 138 also displays the Eastfield West Highland terrier emblem on its bonnet door and a full set of snowploughs at both ends. Occasionally the centre plough was not fitted, for ease of coupling.
Max Fowler

Below:
On 16 May 1978 No 20 002 leads No 20 149 into Crianlarich with a Fort William–Mossend freight. At this time most WHL freight was worked by '20s' and '27s', with the latter in the majority. Although there was no rule, the Scottish Region had a tendency to fold discs upwards rather than downwards when not being displayed, and the region was also more likely to display the correct disc headcode formation, despite the system long having been dispensed with. *Tom Heavyside*

Above:
In 1980 an Eastfield Class 20 was stationed at Fort William to replace the Class 08 for local trip work to the Lochaber aluminium smelter and the paper mill. On 13 August 1987 No 20 225 shunts wagons in the yard. This locomotive had just been transferred from Haymarket, so was probably making its first visit to the West Highlands. The versatility of a '20' over an '08' was demonstrated on several occasions when they deputised for Class 37s on passenger trains, and the following day, No 20 225 worked the 16.10 Fort William–Mallaig and 18.50 return.
Phil Hawkins

Left:
Working flat-out to climb to the summit at Tyndrum on the West Highland line, Nos 20 103 and 20 049 head a southbound freight from Fort William on 17 May 1978. This line still has regular freight, albeit in the hands of General Motors Class 66s.
Tom Heavyside

Heading to Skeggy!

Above:
While most Skegness trains would have attracted a good few 'haulage bashers' in search of a ride behind the usually freight-only machines, the 08.46 Burton–Skegness on 31 May 1982 would have been even more sought after as it was worked by Tinsley-based Nos 20 096 and 20 131 in place of the usual Toton locomotives. Both are still at work, although No 20 131 is now refurbished as No 20 306. *John Tuffs*

Right:
A classic scene witnessed by many a '20' fan in the 1970s and 1980s — waiting at Long Eaton for the returning Skegness–Derby train. On a fine summer Saturday afternoon, No 20 169 leads No 20 045 on the 12.58 from Skegness into the station on 6 June 1981. The snowploughs are most definitely not needed! *Norman Preedy*

Left:
The 12.38 Skegness–Derby arrives at Nottingham, hauled by Nos 20 164 and 20 174 on 9 June 1984. Both retain the old livery variation of cabside BR badges, a feature they would take to the scrapyard and a reminder that they had not been overhauled since 1979. *John Tuffs*

Right:
14 July 1984 was a memorable day on the Skegness line. Nos 20 057 and 20 214 worked the 07.10 from Sheffield — at this time Immingham '20s' on passenger trains were exceptionally rare. However No 20 214 failed near Alfreton and Nos 20 140 and 20 227 took over at Nottingham. On the returning 10.41 from Skegness, No 20 140 failed at Boston and was left in the siding leaving No 20 227 to work bonnet first with 11 coaches to Nottingham where the patched-up Nos 20 214 and 20 057 took over, only for No 20 214 to fail again near Alfreton! Over an hour and a half late, No 20 227 races past Hubberts Bridge. *John Rudd*

Left:
Nos 20 136 and 20 141 pass Sleaford on 14 August 1983 with the 08.56 Derby–Skegness. This day saw eight Class 20s at the resort — just earlier Nos 20 179/191 had passed with the 08.31 from Derby followed by Nos 20 160/180 on the 08.25 from Leicester. However, Nos 20 179/191 failed and returned light to Nottingham while Nos 20 072 and 20 158 ran light to replace them for the 19.15 Skegness–Derby. *John Chalcraft*

Left:
In the summer of 1977 the Saturday Sheffield–Skegness train via Nottingham was worked by pairs of Tinsley Class 20s, but it was not until the summer of 1982 that two '20s' set forth from the steel city for the Lincolnshire resort. Two pairs were used that year, 11 September's use of Tinsley-based Nos 20 105/106 being the highlight. The returning 11.00 from 'Skeggy' approaches Sleaford with No 20 106 leading — and missing its multiple-working jumper cable. *John Chalcraft*

Right:
On 25 August 1984 Nos 20 169 and 20 141 blast past Maud Foster on the outskirts of Boston with the 09.32 from Derby. The first pair of '20s' to reach Skegness from the East Midlands arrived on 7 July 1973 when No D8111 partnered No D8172 on the 09.20 from Derby instead of two '25s'. The following year three pairs made the trip; '20s' — spare at weekends — were liked because the loads were not heavy. In 1975 they became the favoured power for many of the trains, and extended their operations to weekday services. It was to be September 1993 when the last workings to 'Skeggy' were recorded with '20s'. *John Rudd*

Left:
The flatlands of rural Lincolnshire surround Nos 20 173 and 20 088 on the 09.22 Derby–Skegness on 30 August 1980. At the side are allotments growing various produce — unfortunately much more of a rarity nowadays. *Brian Morrison*

Right:
In 1985 mixed pairings of Toton and Tinsley '20s' became slightly more common. On 11 July Tinsley's No 20 088 and Toton's 20 133 made a second consecutive trip to Skegness. Here, having arrived with the 08.48 from Leicester, they have run round and been shut down while they enjoy a long break before returning with the 19.00 to Leicester. *John Tuffs*

Left:
In the mid-1970s, Class 20s occasionally ran to Skegness with 'Jolly Fisherman' headboards, but the board on No 20 125 proclaims the 'Nottingham Class 20 Bashers' and is being displayed to commemorate what, at the time, was expected to be the last booked Class 20-hauled train from the Lincolnshire resort. However, Nos 20 125 and 20 148's departure on the 19.00 to Leicester on 5 May 1986 was not the last and '20s' made sporadic appearances in 1986/7 before regaining a booked duty in 1988 — and it was to be 3 September 1993 that '20s' left 'Skeggy' for the last time on a passenger train. *John Tuffs*

Right:
Photographers get their pictures at Skegness on 18 September 1982 as Nos 20 016 and 20 077 wait to leave with the 12.35 to Leicester — the last visit of the summer season by holiday trains that year.
On 29 August 2007, DRS Nos 20 311/315 visited Skegness on a Railtour, the first 20s in the town on a passenger train for 14 years. *John Chalcraft*

Unusual passenger jobs

Above:
Class 20s occasionally rescued IC125s, but such workings were exceptionally rare. However, one such instance was on 29 April 1987 when Nos 20 197 and 20 169 assisted the 08.33 Plymouth–York from Bristol. The train reached Derby, where it was terminated. *Mike Hodge*

Right:
A train keenly watched by enthusiasts in Scotland was the 12.05 Bristol–Edinburgh, which would often be worked from Carstairs by freight locomotives. In the summer of 1984, with the miners' strike biting hard, the occasional use of Haymarket's '20s' could be enjoyed on the train. Nos 20 205 and 20 223 have just arrived at Edinburgh on 27 July. *Mike Hodge*

Left:
1985 saw major changes to the fleet, and its sphere of operation increased as BR ran down the Class 25 fleet following on from the elimination of the '40s' and '46s'. Unusual WCML passenger work befell three pairs on 1 September as Nos 20 147 and 20 028 wait to leave Bletchley, having been attached to Class 87 electric No 87 020 *North Briton* to drag it to Coventry on the 10.50 Euston-Liverpool. Previous trains had been hauled by Nos 20 041/082, 20 106/130 and No 58 019. *Brian Daniels*

Above:
A rare passenger working for Class 20s was on 27 May 1986 when Nos 20 183 and 20 028 took over the 10.40 Poole–Newcastle at Reading and worked to Birmingham New Street. The train arrives at Coventry off the single-track line from Leamington, via Kenilworth. *Author's collection*

Above:
There is so little left on No 20 059 that you can see right through the cab bulkhead! The locomotive is bereft of bogies and all internal equipment as part of its overhaul at Derby Works on 23 February 1985. It emerged in October in Railfreight grey livery. Its previous overhaul was in July 1980 at Glasgow St Rollox, whose trademark larger eight-inch numerals were applied to overhauled locomotives after November 1979. *Brian Daniels*

Right:
Three crashed '20s' stand in Crewe Works on 12 November 1978 with No 20 081 in front of No 20 033 and No 20 097 to the left — the cab ends being damaged. The smashes on Nos 20 081/097 was slight and both were repaired, but No 20 033 was condemned. *Brian Daniels*

Above:
TOPS renumbering of Class 20s started in 1973, but as No 8000 could not become 20 000, to keep the first 50 together (because of their 526/5D traction motors) it became 20 050; accordingly No 8050 was renumbered 20 128, and No 8128 became 20 228. Because of its historical significance as the first production-series diesel delivered to British Railways, on 18 June 1957, No 20 050 was claimed by the National Railway Museum. It stands at Swindon Works shortly after withdrawal on 14 December 1980. *Brian Daniels*

Below:
St Rollox in Glasgow was responsible for the majority of Class 20 overhauls until 1982 when Crewe, and later Derby, shared the workload as dual-braking started. On 27 September 1980 Toton's No 20 173 is stripped to its frame as part of an overhaul that would be completed in the following November. It was not dual-braked during this work. *Brian Daniels*

Right:
One of the most unusual Class 20 tours was back on 13 August 1978 when Tinsley's No 20 098 was given the less than taxing task of taking F&W Railtours' three-coach 'Tintern Totter'. The Type 1 has just arrived back from Tintern and runs round at Chepstow prior to returning to Worcester via Birmingham. *John Chalcraft*

'Choppers' on tours

Right:
On 15 July 1979 No 20 154 worked one of the more unusual railtours, F&W's 'Severnsider' taking in the freight lines of Tytherington, Sharpness and Gloucester Docks. No 20 154 was working its first passenger train, as, despite being Toton-allocated, it was one of the dual-braked '20s' — never common on Skegness trains before 1983. Withdrawn in 1993, No 20 154 was one of 43 never to work to the resort. *John Chalcraft*

Right:
An unusual working for a '20' was on 7 May 1994 when No 20 227 top-and-tailed with Bo-Bo electric No 12 *Sarah Siddons* on the 'Metro Gnome' tour of Metropolitan lines of the London Underground. The train started at Wembley and visited Chesham, Uxbridge, Amersham and Watford. *Author*

Right:
Meldon Quarry is the unusual setting for Nos 20 169 and 20 184, the pair having arrived on 8 July 1984 with F&W Railtours' 'Devonshire Dart', which saw the debut of the class at Plymouth. Two years later Cornwall was conquered by the '20s'.
Norman Preedy

Right:
On 8 June 1986 F&W Railtours planned to take two '20s' to the end of the line at Penzance for the first time ever. While the train visited Falmouth with Class 37 No 37 207 *William Cookworthy*, Nos 20 011/ 054 went to Long Rock depot for fuel, but the derailment of No 37 196 *Tre Pol and Pen* at Truro meant the charter did not make it to the Cornish terminus. Consequently a repeat attempt was run on 31 August and Nos 20 094/ 124 were successful in making it to the terminus. With No 20 094 leading (and displaying a Wigan pork pie logo!), the ground-breaking '20s' wait to work back to Wolverhampton.
Norman Preedy

Left:
Two of Haymarket's '20s' find themselves in Ayrshire on 10 May 1986 on railtour duty as Nos 20 222 and 20 204 stand at Ardrossan with F&W Railtours' 'Skirl o' the Pipes 7' tour. *Mike Hodge*

Scottish Class 1 work

Above:
No D8081 and a sister arrive at Stirling on a northbound passenger train in 1964, the working not recorded. Both are in green livery — BR blue being a year away from widespread application — although the rear locomotive has gained full yellow ends. *Author's collection*

Below:
One of the rarest Class 20s for passenger work was No 20 111, withdrawn on 22 April 1987. On 1 July 1966 No D8111 works a day excursion from Heads of Ayr to Glasgow Central, and calls at Ayr. *John Chalcraft*

Above:
Throughout their careers, Class 20s have been used to work failed passenger trains. A very interesting rescue mission was on 5 June 1982 when Nos 20 002 and 20 175 — both running bonnet-first — took over the 13.15 Stranraer–Euston at Barassie, near Ayr. It is thought they worked to Carlisle.
Mike McDonald

Left:
In 1990 there was a booked passenger job for a Trainload Coal Class 37 from Ayr to Carlisle and back, but on 26 May it produced its one and only pair of '20s' — with Nos 20 122 and 20 138 given the honours. The 10.40 outward train passes Cockhill, between Barassie and Kilmarnock. They returned at 14.00 from Carlisle. No 20 122 has had its headcode discs removed, a common feature on '20s' overhauled in the mid-1980s.
Robin Ralston

Right:
After a five-year gap, on 31 July 1998 Nos 20 306/310 became the first '20s' to work a main-line service train when they hauled Virgin's 14.35 Euston–Glasgow Central from Carlisle, diverted via the Glasgow Sou' Western route after a landslide on the WCML. The '20s' stand at the blocks with 90 003 *The Herald* in tow. DRS '20s' and '37s' spent the next three days hauling Virgin trains via Dumfries. *Robin Ralston*

Below:
While '20s' occasionally worked passenger trains to Mallaig in the 1980s, working south towards Crianlarich unaided was much rarer. On 13 May 1988 No 20 138 handled the 14.15 Fort William-Glasgow Queen Street and was swapped at Crianlarich for a Class 37 which had arrived on a northbound freight — which No 20 138 then took over. Of added interest is the Civil Engineer's department tool van behind the locomotive. *Ian Nightingale*

Left:
The old British Railways Scottish Region light-blue enamel Mallaig nameboard survived as late as 3 June 1983, albeit having fallen off its posts! No 20 148 waits to run round the 16.05 from Fort William, detach the oil tankers on the rear and hook up for the 18.55 back whence it came. *Les Nixon*

Below:
On the same day, it was typically dull weather on the Mallaig line when No 20 148 made its welcome, if unexpected appearance on the 16.05 Fort William–Mallaig and 18.55 return. The latter passes Morar with the three-coach train no problem for the former Toton locomotive that moved north in July 1982 and was overhauled and dual-braked straight away. The outward working had been with three oil tankers tagged on the back. *Les Nixon*

Mallaig wanderings

Above:
Just two years old, No D8040 rests at its then home depot at Devons Road, Bow, East London, on 27 August 1961. In February 1964 this depot was closed and most of its allocation of '20s' transferred to other London depots such as Stratford, Camden or Willesden. *Bill Hamilton*

Taking a break

Right:
Coalville was a busy focal point for coal operations until the early 1990s, and it was commonplace in the 1970s and 1980s to see several pairs of '20s' stabled at weekends. No 20 177 heads a line of 10 with two Class 56s to the right on 6 April 1980. *Brian Daniels*

Above:
Toton '20s' would be stabled at various depots when not in use, such as Nottingham, Derby, Bescot, Saltley, Coalville, Barrow Hill and Westhouses and at the latter are Nos 20 030 and 20 193 on 27 March 1978. This depot closed in January 1986 as coal traffic declined, partly as a result of the year-long miners' strike in 1984/5.
John Chalcraft

Below:
Wath Yard was one location where diesel was swapped for electric power on trans-Pennine freight trains using the Manchester–Wath–Sheffield 'Woodhead' route. On 6 April 1980 Nos 20 035 and 20 009 are 'on shed' at the nearby Wath depot, which closed in January 1983, not long after the closure of the MSW in July 1981. *Brian Daniels*

Above:
Barrow Hill was a depot where Toton and Tinsley '20s' would often meet in the 1980s, although usually there would be more Eastern locomotives stabled than their Midland sisters. On 6 April 1980 Tinsley's No 20 154 stands in the roundhouse next to Class 08 No 08 868, Class 56 No 56 004 and a Class 47, while on the turntable is Class 37 No 37 169. Barrow Hill is now a major engineering base, and HNRC has several Class 20s based here. *Brian Daniels*

Centre right:
Visitors to Eastfield depot would often be greeted by a line-up of locomotives outside the shed. No 20 207 is flanked by two '08's, a '37' and a '25'. In March 1983 No 20 207 crashed, but it took four months before it was condemned. It then waited another three years before being scrapped, in June 1986. *Brian Daniels*

Right:
On 5 July 2002 Direct Rail Services' Nos 20 306 and 20 311 undergo routine maintenance and exams inside the immaculate Kingmoor depot at Carlisle. This former BR depot was derelict when DRS took it over in 1998 and refurbished it to act as its main depot for its expanding fleet. *Author*

Left:
In the summer of 1992 Thornaby had a fleet of Class 20s for steel traffic, but they were steadily withdrawn except for Nos 20 118/137/165, outbased at Sheffield Tinsley for working local steel trains to Stocksbridge. The trio stands outside the shed in 1992. Nos 20 118 and 20 137 are preserved, while No 20 165 was sold by EWS to DRS in May 2000, stripped and scrapped in December 2001. *J. Porter / Ivan Stewart collection*

Right:
Patched up after a minor bump, No 20 148 rests at its home depot at Toton on 2 April 1978. Class 20s featured all manner of cabside permutations in the 1970s with three different sizes of badge, sometimes above the number, sometimes below. *Danny Preston*

Left:
Despite being BR blue, at least Nos 8077/112 and 20 039/116 spent periods with their numbers in the wrong font. Paired with No 20 100, No 20 116 shows the incorrect style of numbers on shed at Ayr on 11 April 1977. *Danny Preston*

North West operations

Above:
Passing underneath Warrington Bank Quay on 23 February 1985 are Nos 20 158 and 20 134 with an empty coal train from Fiddlers Ferry. The rear locomotive was written off in a collision at Worksop on 18 May 1989 which brought about its premature withdrawal. *Tom Heavyside*

Right:
Two more Toton veterans together on coal duty in the North West, Nos 20 196 and 20 182 pass Warrington Arpley with empty hoppers from Fiddlers Ferry Power Station on 16 May 1988. *Tom Heavyside*

Above:
The first '20s' were sent for driver training at Wigan Springs Branch in 1984 and they remained an everyday sight at the depot until 1992. On shed on 24 April 1990 were Nos 20 133 and 20 194, with snowplough-fitted No 20 131 on the left. *J. Porter / Ivan Stewart collection*

Centre left:
By April 1992 just 11 Class 20s survived in traffic for coal work in the North West pending the last of the Class 60 deliveries. Accordingly they were in demand for charters and other special events, and 25 April saw Nos 20 168 and 20 059 work the 12.52 Manchester Victoria–Barrow in place of a DMU. They then went on to work the 15.32 Barrow–Preston and 17.15 Preston–Liverpool. This train was hauled in connection with an open day at Manchester Longsight depot. *Mel Holley*

Left:
An industrial backdrop as Nos 20 169 and 20 019 head through Warrington Low Level with a coal train on 20 April 1990. In the North West, '20s' worked coal trains from Bickershaw, Silverdale, Parkside and Point of Ayr collieries to the power station at Fiddlers Ferry as well as trains of imported coal from Liverpool. *J. Porter / Ivan Stewart collection*

Right:
When the WCML was closed between Wigan and Preston for engineering work or an accident, trains would be diverted via Lostock Junction, requiring a double reversal. To save time trains would head south from Wigan North Western behind a 'drawback' locomotive with the train locomotive kept on the rear. On 9 September 1984 Nos 20 212/ 219 were used and started a brief five-year association of '20s' on the duties, some of it in the winter. On 28 October the same pair pass Westhoughton with the 09.22 Liverpool–Edinburgh.
Tom Heavyside

On the Lostock diversions

Left:
In the summer of 1985 there were two Class 20 diagrams on the Lostock diversions, and on 30 June No 20 016 leads No 20 001 on the approach to Lostock Junction at the end of their 6½-mile passenger run on the 08.50 Crewe–Blackpool, with No 47 604 on the rear. Both these locomotives were fast approaching their 30th birthday, and 50 years on from delivery to Devons Road, both survive today.
Tom Heavyside

Right:
Lostock Junction on 25 August 1985 sees Nos 20 078 and 20 075 arrive with the 09.22 Liverpool–Edinburgh, which they have worked from Wigan North Western. Train engine No 47 435 will now work forward to Preston.
Paul Shannon

Left:
One of the early withdrawal casualties was No 20 024, which crashed in Mossend yard when it ran away on 2 February 1977 and was written off. From September 1967 to October 1971 No 8024 was allocated to Gateshead and York depots, and on 13 July 1971 the locomotive runs bonnet-first off the Scarborough line at York with a freight for nearby Dringhouses Yard. The locomotive is in green with full yellow ends, and retains steampipes — typical of the fleet at the time. *Norman Preedy*

North Eastern variety

Below:
In 1971 there were two Summer Saturday passenger jobs for York-based Class 20s from Scarborough, the 09.50 to Sheffield, train 1J20, and the 10.05 to Plymouth, train 1V86, which they also worked to Sheffield. On 4 September Nos 8305 and 8305 leave the seaside town with the first train, the nine-coach 1J20, displaying the correct headcode. *Peter Rose*

Right:
One period of Class 20 activity not well recorded was the late 1960s and early 1970s when they were used on the North Eastern — perhaps because the end of steam in 1968 saw many photographers 'retire'. No 8027 passes Aycliffe in County Durham with a lengthy mixed freight in October 1972. *Norman Preedy*

Below:
Another route in the North East that enjoyed Class 20s for a few years in the late 1980s was the Boulby branch with pairs used to haul potash trains. On 12 March 1990 No 20 156 — with the name *HMS Endeavour* painted on its solebar — leads No 20 118 *Saltburn-by-the-Sea* as they head west towards Teesside. *J. Porter / Ivan Stewart collection*

North of the border

Above:
In early 1991, before the end of Speedlink, '20s' were the favoured power for trips to the Cameron Bridge distillery in Fife. Nos 20 165 and 20 118 are engaged in shunting manœuvres that give the appearance of a push-pull freight!
Max Fowler

Left:
On 24 May 1974 No 20 099 is almost ready to leave Kinneil Colliery, near Linlithgow, with a loaded coal train — and will do so once the brake van on the left is attached. Like so much of the country, Scotland's coal mining has been decimated and scenes like this — unfitted and partially fitted trains of coal in mineral wagons — are definitely for the historians and preservationists to cherish.
Tom Heavyside

Right:
When the Westinghouse air brake equipment was removed from Nos 20 085/086 both retained one hose as a through air pipe should the locomotives be coupled inside a dual-braked locomotive on an air-braked train. No 20 086 stands at the now-closed Frances Colliery, at Dysart near Kirkcaldy in Fife on 24 May 1974 next to a 1949-built NCB colliery steam locomotive.
Tom Heavyside

Left:
A regular turn that took Class 20s to the central Highlands was the Bowling–Invergordon oil-tank train. On 13 June 1980 Nos 20 156 and 20 152 take the station-avoiding line at Rose Street Junction as they avoid Inverness station and head for the Far North line. Weedkilling trains apart, it is thought no '20s' have ever been to either Kyle of Lochalsh or north of Invergordon. *Tom Heavyside*

Right:
Pilot Scheme No 20 011 arrives at Glasgow Central with the empty stock for the up travelling post office to London on 23 May 1974. In the intervening 17 years from delivery, the former No D8011 has lost its oval buffers for round replacements and been dual-braked. The cabside shows the typical livery of the time with large BR double arrows above the number and the data panel at the bottom.
Tom Heavyside

Left:
A classic railway scene — a train coming off the Forth Bridge heading south at Dalmeny. On 14 June 1983 Nos 20 198 and 20 216 trundle a featherweight load of just one bogie van towards Edinburgh. *John Chalcraft*

Below:
Throughout the 1970s, Class 20s were the prime power for coal trains in Fife, working mainly in pairs. On 17 April 1978 Nos 20 216/225 pass Dunfermline with a loaded coal train, with the brake van behind the locomotives. At this time dual-braked Nos 20 179/184/191/203/216-227 were allocated to Haymarket depot in Edinburgh for such traffic, but spent most of their spare time stabled at Thornton Junction or Townhill depots. *Brian Daniels*

Above:
When the first blue repaints were undertaken by Scottish works, the full-height nose-end yellow panel did not wrap round the side. In this 11 September 1971 picture at Polmadie, No 8110 brings up the rear of a short convoy with Nos 8117 and 8090 leading. No 8117 has its number on its bodyside while No 8090 has a bigger badge compared with No 8110. *Norman Preedy*

Centre Right:
Inverness depot was home to a handful of '20s' in the early 1960s — from January 1960 to October 1966 and from June 1979 to February 1980 when Nos 20 007/ 020/085 were allocated. However, the type were semi-regular visitors until 1990, and on Sunday 8 September 1985 Eastfield's Nos 20 201 and 20 156 were stabled in the sidings prior to heading south the next day. No 20 201 was one of the first to be given a headlight, and differed by having a visible connecting cable to the lamp. *J. Porter / Ivan Stewart collection*

Right:
With '20s', '26s', '37s' and '47s' stabled on Millerhill depot, No 20 202 runs nose first into the yard with a lengthy mixed freight on 13 August 1982. *John Chalcraft*

Matlock DMU replacements

Left:
Class 20 followers enjoyed an unusual and unexpected bonus in 1990 when the type found use on Derby–Matlock local services. At first pairs were used nose-to-nose, but the time lost running round — especially at Matlock, with the need to use the loop north of the station — meant the operation was far from ideal. After a few days, dispensation was given to run the '20s' top-and-tail. On 2 August No 20 058 is at Derby on the rear of the 11.20 to Matlock, headed by No 20 087. This duo were no strangers to top-and-tail operations, as in 1986 they were fitted with remote multiple working to work MGR trains in this fashion, a trial never pursued. *John Tuffs*

Below:
Later the same day, the 12.42 Derby–Matlock passes Duffield with No 20 058 on the rear. 23 Class 20s appeared on these workings on an *ad hoc* basis when DMUs were unavailable. *John Tuffs*

Above:
A train keenly watched by enthusiasts in the late 1970s was 1M60, the 15.15 Plymouth–Manchester which re-engined at Gloucester using the traction from a Bescot–Gloucester freight, occasionally a pair of '20s'. On 3 July 1979 Nos 20 197 and 20 044 have backed on, but dragging brakes saw No 20 197 catch fire at Cheltenham, so Class 45/0 No 45 070 took over. Class 20s worked train 1M60 on 32 occasions from 1978 to 1980. *Norman Preedy*

"Has 1M60 got '20s' tonight?"

Left:
Another shot of train 1M60, the 15.15 Plymouth–Manchester, as it waits to leave Gloucester with Tinsley's No 20 112 leading No 20 046 on 6 July 1979. This train occasionally got '20' power even in the deep winter — a few months later, on 18 December, Nos 20 010 and 20 046 did the honours. These two performances notwithstanding, No 20 046 was to work just one more passenger train, in 1980, despite lasting in traffic until 1992. *Norman Preedy*

Left:
One of the more unusual mixed pairings to feature a Class 20 is that with a Class 45 'Peak', especially an ETH variant. However, on 21 January 1986 No 20 057 was needed to assist ailing No 45 124 on a Hams Hall– Drakelow empty fly ash train, and passes Branston, Burton on Trent. When Toton Class 20s were taken to or from Glasgow for overhaul in the 1970s, often it was via hitching a ride on a freight over the Settle–Carlisle line, usually hauled by '40s' or '45/0s', but in such instances, the '20' would be dead. *John Tuffs*

Mixing it about

Above:
A very rare combination indeed — a Class 20 piloting a '33'. D6518 had failed at Hitchin on 21 March 1966 while hauling the returning Uddingston–Cliffe empty cement tanks and a '20' was attached to assist, probably just to clear the lines and take the train to the next yard where space was available to wait for a more suitable replacement. Sadly the Class 20's identity is not recorded by the photographer, but inevitably it is one of the then 34G Finsbury Park allocation. *Peter Chapman*

Right:
More West Highland freight activity, but this time a mixed pair of No 20 115 leading No 27 044 on an unfitted train comprising sheeted 16-tonne mineral wagons. The northbound train is approaching the summit at Tyndrum on 17 May 1978. No 20 115 suffered a collision in 1972 which saw its cab rebuilt — thus despite being one of the original Scottish locomotives, it has the shallower cabside windows. *Tom Heavyside*

Right:
An unexpected passenger duty for '20s' came about in 1983 when used to pilot the Euston-Stranraer 'sleeper' from Ayr to combat slipping on the Class 47s on poor railhead conditions. The locomotive, invariably an Eastfield machine, would usually run light back, but sometimes piloted the 07.32 Stranraer-Glasgow to Ayr. On 7 October 1985 No 20 138 has just led No 47 466 from the Galloway town and is uncoupled before returning to more usual freight work.
Alan Evans

Right:
The 07.39 Dundee-Glasgow Queen Street calls at Stirling with No 20 175 leading failed No 25 023 on 23 June 1980. No 20 175 had a fairly interesting career, but it ended in August 1993 after a stint as one of 20 used on tracklaying duties in the Channel Tunnel. It was sold to DRS, but not selected for overhaul; instead, along with No 20 113 it donated parts to the overhaul of other '20s' and was eventually stripped beyond repair and scrapped in December 2003.
Norman Preedy

Nose-first

Above:
No 20 137 runs nose-first with over 30 wagons in tow past Thornton Junction in Fife on 14 June 1983. In such operation Class 20s must be double-manned with the secondman assisting the driver in signal sighting. This was not ideal, and even from an early stage the common nose-to-nose combination soon became the norm. No 20 137 was one of the early '20s' to be dual-braked, in 1971, and is now preserved at the Gloucestershire–Warwickshire Railway. *John Chalcraft*

Right:
At Glasgow Queen Street on 4 July 1986 is No 20 201, but this is not an ECS. The need to turn the 08.30 Inverness–Bristol Temple Meads means the Type 1 is given a rare 2½-mile passenger jaunt to take the train to Cowlairs where it can turn on the triangle to head south. *Al Pulford*

Left:
An unusual and taxing job for bonnet-first No 20 156 on 1 May 1987 is this 10-coach ECS move from Liverpool Lime Street to Derby Etches Park, on the last few miles at Willington. No 20 156 was one of 20 painted in Railfreight livery after overhaul at Glasgow in January 1986. It had a varied career: new to Toton in 1966, it was dual-braked in 1971 and enjoyed spells at Tinsley, Haymarket, Immingham, Eastfield, Motherwell and Thornaby — all main depots associated with the type. It was withdrawn from Eastfield in July 1991 after the end of Speedlink services. *John Tuffs*

Right:
The railway line through Alloa was due to re-open in 2008, but it is doubtful if many Class 20s will visit the line. Back on 18 June 1980 Haymarket '20s' working from Dunfermline Townhill would have been the typical traction on the line from Kincardine, and No 20 218 runs bonnet-first with an empty westbound coal train from one of the local collieries. *Tom Heavyside*

Right:
It's just one locomotive, one van, one brake van as vacuum-braked No 20 102 heads through Edinburgh Waverley on 24 June 1981. Most freight bypasses the city's main station by virtue of the 'sub' line running to the south of the station. *John Chalcraft*

Above:
Trains don't come shorter than this — just one SPA wagon! No 20 075 *Sir William Cooke* stands at Kingswinford Junction signalbox on 25 September 1996 with the 6G75 Brierley Hill–Bescot trip — a very unusual working for a BRT '20' and thought to be a one-off. By this time the only '20s' at work on the main line were the six Hunslet Barclay machines and the four BRT locomotives, although the latter were used in the main by Transrail and, later, EWS. *Andy Williams*

Working in communications

Left:
A delightful picture of Nos 20 075 *Sir William Cooke* and 20 128 *Guglielmo Marconi* in the loop at Bloxwich with the 6T45 trip to Washwood Heath on 8 June 1995. The BRT Class 20s had only just taken over this trip, and this was one of the first workings. The BR Telecommunications Sector took 13 Class 20s, and after No 20 106 was used for spares to overhaul Nos 20 075/128/131/187 the remaining eight, Nos 20 007/032/072/104/117/121/190/215, were stored until sold to DRS. Nos 20 104/117/190 were overhauled to become Class 20/3s, while No 20 007 was preserved and the remainder sold to HNRC. *Andy Williams*

Right:
Local freight occupies Nos 20 128 and 20 075 on 29 June 1995 as they amble past Ryecroft, near Walsall with the 6T45 Washwood Heath–Bescot trip, the rear four TTA wagons for repairs. The four BRT Class 20s were overhauled in 1992/3 and released in BR blue with BRT logos. In 1994 all were repainted in this uninspiring grey livery and named after people associated with telecommunications. No 20 131 was the first, *Almon B. Strowger* at Waterloo on 2 March, followed by Nos 20 075 *Sir William Cooke* and 20 187 *Sir Charles Wheatstone* at Pickering on 28 May and finally No 20 128 *Guglielmo Marconi* at Marylebone on 12 September. *Andy Williams*

Below:
Actually working a train they were intended for, Nos 20 128 and 20 075 climb away from Ryecroft on 13 May 1996 with a BRT train from Bescot to Beeston, Nottingham. From the summer of 1995 until Easter 1997 the operational BRT '20s' were based at Bescot and used by Transrail and later EWS when not required on their occasional BRT duties. Both Nos 20 131 and 20 187 both spent long intervals out of use at Crewe Works in this period, leaving Nos 20 075 and 20 128 to keep the flag flying for Class 20/0s on the main line. *Andy Williams*

Left:
On 1 August 1996 the last operational '20/0' in traffic was No 20 075, working off Bescot depot. That night it was used for a most unusual duty for a '20' — the structure-gauging train — and also on a line not familiar territory for the type — Stratford-on-Avon. The Type 1 stands in the station having just propelled the train from Hatton. *Mike Gregory*

Below:
By virtue of their blue-star multiple-working system, Class 20s could work with many other BR classes. On 9 August 1995 No 20 075 *Sir William Cooke* was with Class 37 No 37 201 *Saint Margaret* on the 7G07 Bescot–Honeybourne spoil train and passes Lower Moor, between Norton Junction and Evesham on the Cotswold line. The train had been booked for the '37', but the heavy load saw the crew request the added power from the '20'. *Andy Williams*

Foursomes

Above:
In 1990 some coal trains from Gladstone Dock, Liverpool were deemed too heavy for a single pair of Class 20s to get up the 1-in-60 climb at Bootle Junction. Accordingly, a pilot pair of '20s' were added. Railfreight grey No 20 141 and Pilot Scheme No 20 016 have been added to lead Nos 20 128/168 on an MGR train for Fiddlers Ferry Power Station on 2 May. *J. Porter / Ivan Stewart collection*

Right:
It is not known for what reason Tinsley's Nos 20 106 and 20 128 are piloting Toton's Nos 20 185 and 20 181, but it is assumed at least one of the latter has failed. The train is a down mixed freight at Treeton, Sheffield, on 30 June 1982. *Tom Heavyside*

Left:
In the early 1980s, Haymarket's No 20 203 was given a unique front with a yellow headcode plate similar to those fitted to Class 37s and Class 55s. It ambles through Inverkeithing on 29 August 1986 with a northbound infrastructure train, a typical duty for the type at this time. *Barry Adams*

Nose jobs

Left:
Prior to the BRT fleet, Haymarket's No 20 219 was the only '20' with a nose-end high-intensity headlight. The rather crude, and off-centre, attachment is shown at Inverkeithing on 21 August 1986. *Brian Daniels*

Left:
Two Scottish Class 20s, No D8085/6, were fitted with Westinghouse air-brake equipment to move EMU stock to Yoker depot, and the extra pipes are clearly visible on No 8085 at Glasgow Central on 9 May 1972. The equipment was soon removed, with No 20 086 dual-braked in 1976 and No 20 085 in 1984. Still retaining its through steampipe, the buffer-beam is fairly cluttered. *Tom Heavyside*

Right:
In 1982 severe snow in Scotland rendered three-piece miniature snowploughs ineffective, such was the height of some drifts. To combat heavier snowfalls, several Eastfield '20s' were fitted with Bielhack ploughs, which were attached to the locomotives by removing the buffers and using the mounting bolts. The '20s' were coupled cab-to-cab in pairs and sent on patrols as required. No 20 028 stands at Eastfield depot with No 20 099. *Richard Howat*

Below:
Despite being just 1,000hp, Class 20s were often given some impressive loads to haul. It is as late — or as early! — as 3 August 1977, yet snowploughs are still fitted to No 20 117 as it shunts a lengthy train of vans loaded with whisky at Kilmarnock. The locomotive's horn grille is missing on the cab roof. *Danny Preston*

Snowploughs

Above:
English Electric used the Class 20 as the basis for the 1,350hp Class 1400 locomotive for Portuguese Railways Comboios de Portugal (CP), which ordered 67. The first 10, Nos 1401-10, were built by EE at Vulcan Foundry while the remaining 57 were built under licence by Sorefame. On 27 January 2007 Nos 1408 and 1411 stand at Valença on the northern border with Spain with a return special to Porto for the UK-based Portuguese Traction Group. *Author*

The '1400s' – the Portuguese Class 20s

Right:
CP No 1424 stands at Pamphilosa on 28 January 2007 repainted in original deep blue livery. This side view shows the similarities of the bogies between the '1400s' and the '20s' and the bodyside door and grille arrangements. The '1400' worked secondary passenger trains and freight through much of the country, but by 2007 just 27 remained in traffic with CP, although 15 had been exported to Argentina. *Author*

Right:
Class 20s were the first main-line British diesel type to find work abroad, first in France on Channel Tunnel tracklaying duties in 1992. That year also saw BR sell four to Chemins de Fer Départementaux for use on freight traffic between Cravant Bazarnes, Étang and Montchanin in the central region of the country. The locomotives, Nos 20 035/063/139/228, were all overhauled at Crewe and shipped out by road. The former Nos 20 035 and 20 063, now CFD Nos 2001/2, amble through Annay on 7 July 1999 with an Autun-bound freight. *Keith Fender*

Below:
The '20s' proved popular with crews and, of course, were reliable. It was only when CFD was taken over in 2002 that their days were numbered and they were replaced by ex-SNCF power. On 7 August CFD Nos 2003/4 run round their train at Saulieu. The overhaul of the CFD '20s' saw them lose their vacuum brakes and have other minor modifications. *Kim Fullbrook*

Above:
It took until 8 August 1998 for British enthusiasts to sample the CFD '20s' on a passenger train in France when a tour arranged by Along Different Lines used CFD Nos 2003/4 from Auxerre to Étang and back — a round trip of 200 miles. In blazing hot weather the train makes a run past at Cravant Bazarnes. On 16 October 1999 a second tour ran using CFD Nos 2001/2 from Auxerre to Cer-la-Tour, returning via Clamency. *Author*

Right:
A good shot of RFS No 2020, formerly No 20 095, shows the exhaust scrubbers fitted to the Channel Tunnel '20s'. Exhaust fumes are collected in the van behind the locomotives and so are not emitted into the tunnel, thus creating an unworkable environment. *David Haydock*

Below:
On 3 November 1992 a track-laying train emerges from the Channel Tunnel at Coquelles in France with Nos 2012 and 2020 in charge. As well as the 20 RFS locomotives, several '20s' were hired from BR, namely Nos 20 087/138 and 20 066/119. No 2012 was No 20 048 and one of five preserved '20s' hired for the track laying project, while No 2020 was sold to DRS after its Channel Tunnel work was over and was overhauled in 1995 and runs today as No 20 305. *David Haydock*

Left:
Pictures of '20s' at work inside the Channel Tunnel are exceptionally rare, but this is No 2011 deep underground and hard at work close to the French end of the tunnel near Coquelles. The former No 20 001 was one of five hired by RFS from preservation groups, and No 20 001 has returned to a more relaxing life at the Midland Railway, Butterley, where it celebrated its 50th birthday on 13 July 2007. *David Haydock*

Centre left:
The Channel Tunnel Rail Link from St Pancras to Folkestone was built in two stages. Section one from Fawkham Junction to the tunnel was started in October 1998 and opened in 2004. Part of its construction saw six Class 20s hired to Victa Railfreight from preservation groups for use on the trains needed for installing the overhead line equipment. Nos 20 001/048/142/188/189/227 were all hired, and on 4 October 2002 No D8188 pauses at Chilson Park while engineers fix the OLE in place. *David Staines*

Below left:
Showing its Metropolitan Railway maroon off to good effect, No 20 227 *Sir John Betjeman* stands at Sandling, in Kent, with an electrification train on 14 February 2003. This locomotive, the last '20' built, was repainted back into Railfreight grey livery in 2006. *Kim Fullbrook*

Right:
Usually based at the Llangollen Railway, No D8142 was one of the CTRL sextet and 22 June 2002 found the machine at Westwell Leacon near Ashford. Soon afterwards this line would be open to 186mph Eurostars — so the chances of a 75mph 1966-built freight engine are sadly never to be repeated. *David Staines*

Above:
Under the still-energised wires of the soon to close Manchester–Sheffield Woodhead route, Nos 20 210 and 20 105 pass Woodburn Junction, Sheffield, with a short wagonload freight on 19 May 1981. Both locomotives are allocated to Tinsley. *John Chalcraft*

Below:
A picture that oozes atmosphere; on 24 February 1981 No 20 112 arrives at the exchange sidings at Elsecar and passes Nos 20 103/129 waiting to leave with a coal train. In the background, two dual-braked Class 76s run light to Wath. All these three Tinsley machines have been scrapped. *John Chalcraft*

Left:
Although five years old by the time this photograph was taken on 6 October 1962 at Willesden depot, No D8006 was still in original livery without yellow warning panels. In October 1958 this locomotive had made the type's debut in Scotland within a month's trial at Kittybrewster depot. It was deemed successful, and Nos D8028-34/70-134 were delivered to Scottish depots in the years 1959-62, to be followed in 1967/8 by Nos D8316-27. Renumbered 20 006 in March 1974, this locomotive would be condemned on 2 October 1990 and scrapped in June 1991.

Class 20s in colour

Above:
This undated 1961 shot shows new No D8058 at Sheffield Victoria, not long after the locomotive was delivered from Darlington to Darnall depot. It sports a bodyside ladder fitted to Nos D8000-127, but this was soon removed following concerns over people climbing on locomotives while under live overhead wires — such as here. On 24 June that year No D8058 became what is thought to be the first Class 20 to visit Skegness, on an excursion from Sheffield. *Peter Rose*

Left:
A comparison of noses! Two of Toton's large allocation of '20s' rest at Nottingham depot on a sunny Sunday Valentine's Day 1982 while two Class 45s in the background show a much different nose end. Both designs, however, are later developments of Pilot Scheme types. *Brian Daniels*

Above:
Unlike other classes, minor livery variations were relatively few on Class 20s in the blue era. One that was undertaken was on Motherwell's No 20 122 which has a grey cab roof applied. The locomotive is stabled at Larbert on 7 August 1982 along with a Class 27/2. *Mike Hodge*

Left:
Another view of a Class 20 undergoing a thorough rebuild, with No 20 132 being rebuilt at Derby on 23 February 1985. The overhauled EE 8SVT engine has been refitted and soon the locomotive will be repainted, becoming the second in Railfreight livery. *Brian Daniels*

Right:
In the 1970s, Class 20s were semi-regulars on the Highland main line, and even occasionally worked passenger trains. However, on 2 August No 20 126 arrived at Inverness piloting Nos 26 019/022 on the 21.50 overnight 'sleeper' from London Euston. It is not known where the '20' was attached, most likely at Aviemore to assist over Slochd, presumably because one of the '26s' had failed.
Dave Howlett

Below:
On 29 July 1978 the 13.10 Glasgow Queen Street–Inverness was worked by Nos 20 121/126 instead of a Class 40 or two Class 26s. At Aviemore, No 20 121 failed and was detached, leaving No 20 126 to carry on solo to Carrbridge. In the meantime Inverness dispatched No 40 081 to assist for the five-mile climb at 1-in-60 to the summit at Slochd. Equally remarkable was the 17.05 return to Glasgow being worked by Nos 20 108/110!
Dave Howlett

Left:
In 1984 a nationwide strike by the National Union of Mineworkers deprived BR of much coal traffic, leading to freight locomotives being spare. Haymarket had few qualms about using them on passenger trains in the Edinburgh area, especially on the 'portions' to Carstairs. On 26 May No 20 009 leads No 20 175 with the 16.10 to Carstairs. *Robin Ralston*

Above:
From 31 July 1989 for two weeks, Class 20s 'took over' the Derby–Crewe line, with two of the three DMU diagrams turned over to pairs hauling three coaches. Apart from the odd substitutions by a '31' or '47', the 'Choppers' were the mainstay of the route and this was the only time in the class's history when it was possible to get off one Class 20-hauled train and onto another for the whole of a day! Nos 20 099 and 20 218 pass Tutbury & Hatton with the 11.08 Crewe–Derby on 5 August. The leading locomotive features the Civil Engineers' branding of a small yellow cabside stripe. *Andy Williams*

No coverage of the Skegness line would be complete without the delightful old GNR somersault signals. On 14 June 1986 No 20 032 leads No 20 039, the latter making its one and only appearance on a Skegness passenger train, past Havenhouse with the 07.10 from Sheffield. At this time Class 20s had no booked work to Skegness, but from 14 June this train was hauled fairly regularly by '20s', as were the 09.32 ex Derby and 13.50 ex Grantham. 1987 was a very poor year, just three pairs making it to Skegness, but 1988 saw a booked job return. *Martin Loader*

Right:
Empty stock work was a feature for Class 20s from the start of their career, especially at the London termini at Euston and King's Cross. In the 1970/80s they were used on such duties at Glasgow Central and Queen Street stations. On 25 May 1986 at Central, having brought in a rake of Mk 3 coaches for a London train, is No 20 193, sporting a full set of snowploughs on No 1 end — relatively unusual for a '20'. Introduction of driving van trailers in the late 1980s rendered such moves redundant. *Al Pulford*

Above:
In 1986 a small batch of Class 20s were transferred to Thornaby and one duty was limestone trains on the scenic Redmire line through Wensleydale. On 11 November 1986 Nos 20 173 *Wensleydale* and 20 172 *Redmire* stand at the end of the line with a train for Redcar. *Peter J. Robinson*

Left:
Nos 20 213 and 20 165 near Longannet after unloading a coal train at Kincardine Power Station. At just 73 tonnes each, Class 20s had a versatile route availability of 5, making them the lightest of any main-line locomotives and enabling them to cover all but the most restrictive of lines. *Robin Ralston*

Right:
One of the most famous railtours ever was the Class 20 Locomotive Society's 'Three to the Sea' on 2 May 1987 taking a triple-header to Brighton. Specially for the trip, Tinsley painted Nos 20 030/064 green, although with many differences from the original BR livery, it became known as *Tinsley Green*. They were named *River Rother* and *River Sheaf* respectively and the third — ex-works No 20 118 — was named *'River Don'*. Surrounded by SR EMUs, the trio stand at Brighton prior to returning north.
Barry Adams

Below:
Cockwood Harbour, near Dawlish, a classic location for railway photographers for decades, has only seen a handful of pairs of Class 20s on passenger work — all on railtours. On 2 May 1994 Nos 20 118 and 20 131 *Almon B. Strowger* head north with the 17.10 Paignton–York Pathfinder Tours' 'Torbay Exe-Cursioner' charter which they worked to Derby. *Martin Loader*

Above:
An unexpected charter job befell two of Eastfield's RETB-fitted Class 20s on 28 May 1988 when Nos 20 127 and 20 114 took over an SRPS Gourock–Mallaig charter at Dumbarton and worked to Fort William. The train passes the famous Horseshoe Curve near Bridge of Orchy. They returned through to Gourock. *Robin Ralston*

Left:
Passing one of the few surviving semaphore signal gantries at Llandudno are Railfreight grey No 20 215 and BR blue No 20 142 on 8 August 1991. They have arrived with the 08.11 from Derby and are propelling out to the run-round loop. They will then stable until the 16.44 return departure time. *Barry Adams*

Above:
An unusual duty for BRT Nos 20 075 and 20 128 occurred on 24 May 1995 when they top-and-tailed train 1Z15, the 08.40 Derby RTC–Walsall test train. It passes Litchurch Lane at the start of the journey. *Paul Robertson*

Right:
Despite 101 Class 20s being scrapped, one survived the MC Metals onslaught, No 20 189. It was found in 1990 that the company's yard shunter was insufficient to move 136-tonne Class 45s so No 20 189 was resurrected to take its place. Repainted grey, after the yard ceased operating in 1999, it was sold to Michael Owen.
On 23 September 1995 No 20 189 made its only appearance away from MCM when it starred at the Bo'ness & Kinneil Railway's diesel gala. It waits to head to Birkhill. *Author*

Left:
In BR days, only one Class 20 was painted in two-tone grey livery, No 20 088. In 1987 classified overhauls had finished, but the following year several were sent to Doncaster works for maintenance too major to be carried out at depots, but just No 20 088 was repainted. Although it was part of the Trainload Coal fleet, the appropriate symbols were not added. In 2005 two-tone grey was adopted by HNRC and Nos 20 096/901/905 are so painted, while in preservation, No 20 031 also carries this livery. With original Railfreight grey No 20 163 for company, No 20 088 rests at Coalville on 2 June 1990. *A. O. Wynn*

Above:
In 1989 and again in 1991 Class 20s had booked passenger work to Llandudno from Derby and the Potteries, and 52 different '20s' made it to the town in these two years alone. On 8 August 1991 Nos 20 142 and 20 215 wait for their 16.44 departure time back to Derby. *Barry Adams*

Above:
Waterman Railways bought Nos 20 042/188 in 1993 and painted them in its black livery. Neither were main line certified, so were only used occasionally at heritage railways. On 11 July 1997 No 20 042 has arrived at Bury Bolton Street piloting Class 50 No 50 033 *Glorious* on the 19.00 from Rawtenstall. This machine was sold to DRS and is now in traffic as No 20 312, while No 20 188 is preserved at the Swanage Railway. *Author*

Below:
A picture that shows the Central Services livery to great effect as No 20 169 and Railfreight grey No 20 118 stand at Skegness with the 18.12 to Leicester on 28 July 1993, the last year Class 20s worked passenger trains to the resort. No 20 118 has lost its BR badge as its doors have been repainted. Both '20s' are preserved. *Barry Adams*

Left:
An exceptionally unusual place to find Class 20s is Marylebone station in West London and firmly in former Great Central Railway territory! On 7 December 1994 BRT Nos 20 075 and 20 128 have arrived with the tribometer train and are waiting to work over LUL lines to Uxbridge and Rickmansworth. *Paul Robertson*

Below:
Resting outside their home depot at Carlisle Kingmoor on 5 July 2002 are Nos 20 310 and 20 313. Unlike in their BR days, as a rule the DRS fleet is usually very clean. At this time the 10 Wabtec '20s' were instantly recognisable from their Brush counterparts by virtue of a cab-end multiple-working socket, a feature since retro-fitted to Nos 20 301-305. *Author*

Above:
Unlike in the UK, the sun usually shone on the Class 20s when working in France! On 6 August 1998 CFD Nos 2003 (ex-20 139) and 2004 (ex-20 228) pass a French DMU as they shunt in the yard at Avallon. *Kim Fullbrook*

Below:
Painted in a striking orange, white and turquoise livery, the CFD '20s' had headcodes removed and featured new light clusters, but they were unmistakable! They worked for the best part of a decade with no overhauls. The first was laid up in 1998, but CFD No 2004 worked until 2002. On 6 August 1998 CFD Nos 2003 and 2004 pass Brecy with the daily Cravant Bazarnes–Saulieu freight. *Kim Fullbrook*

Above:
At work on the Channel Tunnel Rail Link Section 1 electrification on 31 January 2003 is No D8048. Owned by the Midland Class 20 Association, the well-travelled '20' stands at Singlewell, near Gravesend, in the snow. *Kim Fullbrook*

Below:
There is a certain kind of pleasure in seeing a 1957-built locomotive used on the latest enhancement to the UK's rail system — a 186mph line connecting London with mainland Europe. Pilot Scheme No D8001 stands near the North Downs Tunnel near the village of Detling, on 18 February 2003 with another of the many electrification trains. The locomotive looks all the more authentic for being that bit work-stained. *Kim Fullbrook*

Above:
Nos D8048 and D8098 approach Quorn with a rake of
16-tonne mineral wagons on 28 January 2006, creating
an authentic 1960s train to fit in with the railway's
image. No D8098 was one of the first preserved Class
20s, moving to the Great Central Railway on 22 May
1992 and was repainted in British Railways green the
following year. No D8048 joined it from May 2005 to
June 2007 having had spells at PeakRail, Ruddington
and the Battlefield Line. *Mike Wild*

Above:
In 2006 Class 20s found a new use in industry when
Harry Needle Railroad Company hired two machines
to Corus at Scunthorpe. Initially Nos 20 901/904
were sent to allow staff to become familiar with the
locomotives while Nos 20 056/066 were fully
overhauled and modified for use at the internal rail site
that produces steel — including rail products.
On 29 July 2006 No 20 901, still in DRS blue, stands
at the steelworks' locomotive depot. *Paul Bigland*

Left:
The first HNRC Class 20 overhauled for Corus was
No 20 056, outshopped at Barrow Hill in July 2006
in yellow with a deep red solebar and silver cabsides.
Minor external modifications were new light clusters,
cabside door windows and roof-mounted orange
flashing lights. Numbered 81, the former Tinsley
machine would have been a regular at Barrow Hill
in its BR days but ended its career at Toton in 1990.
It was sold in 1991 for preservation at the Caledonian
Railway but had a spell on hire to RFS. It moved to
Brechin in 1993 but was sold in 1995. It spent June
2003 to October 2005 on hire to Lafarge at Earles
before sale to HNRC. *Author*

A superb picture of No 20 168 *Sir George Earle* at work at the Hope cement works in Derbyshire. Owned by HNRC, the locomotive sports the unique livery of Lafarge/Blue Circle and also features a nose-mounted camera to allow single-manning even when running bonnet-first. It has also had its engine silenced, losing the characteristic whistle for the benefit of local residents. It arrived in October 2004 to replace No D8056 which first appeared at the site in 2003 to work from the exchange sidings at Earles to the cement works, a short 1¼-mile branch, with a stiff gradient of 1-in-50. *Les Nixon*

Right:
The first 128 Class 20s were built with through steampipes for occasional use with boiler-fitted locomotives. The pipes were rarely used, so when 100 extra '20s' were ordered in 1966 these were omitted. Progressively the pipe attachments were removed, and when a loco was dual-braked, the pipe was removed. However, even as late as 1978 No 20 052 retained its hoses, which are to the bottom left of the right-hand buffer in this view at Frodingham on 14 May 1978. *Brian Daniels*

Steampipes

Below:
In 1983 the through steampipes made a brief comeback on two '20s'. Class 37s were experiencing wheelslip problems on the Glasgow–Fort William 'sleeper', especially on Monday mornings when rails were greasy following no traffic on the Sunday nights. This led to Nos 20 045/085 having the hoses refitted to work in multiple with steam-heat '37s'. On 2 June 1983 Nos 37 188 and 20 045 pause at Upper Tyndrum with the 06.00 Glasgow Queen Street–Mallaig, which they will work to Fort William. *Dave Howlett*

Another view of '20s' at work on the heavy Peak Forest limestone trains, with Nos 20 162 and 20 164 in action on 26 August 1984. These two machines were dual-braked in 1971 before the modification was adopted fleet-wide on the type between 1982 and 1986. The PHV wagons were built in 1930-50s yet ended traffic on 31 December 1997 — the last vacuum-braked freight wagons in regular use. *John Chalcraft*

Peak performers

Above:

Nos 20 077 and 20 170 pass Chinley on 9 June 1984 with a limestone train. Both are vacuum-braked — and would remain as two of the last five to be dual-braked in 1985/86. Mass withdrawals of Class 25s and 40s in the early 1980s saw Class 20s take over many of their duties in the North West, including these trains from Buxton. No 20 077 was withdrawn prematurely after an accident at Bickershaw Colliery on 16 March 1988 saw coal dropped onto its cab. *John Chalcraft*

Right:

In 1986 eight Class 20s were renumbered into the '20 3xx' series as they had modified triple valves for working the vacuum-braked ICI limestone trains in the Peak Forest area. Nos 20 302 (previously 20 059) and 20 308 (20 196) pass the closed station at Cheadle with the 6F43 17.43 Tunstead–Oakleigh on 19 June. The renumberings were short-lived, and a pool of newly refurbished Class 37/5s were acquired for these workings, so in November they reverted to their original TOPS numbers, bar No 20 304, which was in works and did not emerge again until March 1987. *Paul Shannon*

Right:
In the early autumn of 1989, its first year working for Hunslet Barclay, No 20 906 *Georgina* brings up the rear of a weedkiller train at Ryecroft Junction near Walsall. No 20 902 *Lorna* is on the front. At this time Nos 20 905 *Iona* and 20 906 were usually the spare locomotives in the fleet, with Nos 20 901 *Nancy* and 20 904 *Janis* usually one pair and Nos 20 902 and 20 903 *Alison* the other pair for the two weedkilling trains that covered the whole of the BR network. *Andy Williams*

Below:
Class 20s had only visited Cornwall twice in BR days before their regular use on the weedkilling train, and both visits were on railtours. Therefore Lostwithiel is not a place widely associated with the type. No 20 901 *Nancy*, with No 20 904 *Janis* out of sight on the rear, has just returned from an amble along the delightful Fowey branch on 4 April 1991. They will spend the best part of a week in the Duchy, visiting all the freight and passenger lines, spraying chemicals to reduce the growth of weeds in the trackbed. *Tom Heavyside*

Killer mooses!

Right:
On 10 March 1990 BR piloted No 47 422 on the 06.34 Carlisle–Leeds with Hunslet Barclay's Nos 20 906 *Georgina* and 20 905 *Iona*. The reason was to attract enthusiasts and followed the use of Nos 20 061/093 the previous November which saw over 1,200 passengers on board. The train waits to leave Carlisle at dawn. *Denzil Morgan*

Below:
Class 20 visits to Skegness post 1993 have been restricted to forays by the weedkilling train and a 2007 railtour. On 7 August 1997, four years after the end of passenger workings by the type to Skegness, Nos 20 903 *Alison* and 20 902 *Lorna* pass the wonderful signalbox at Heckington as they head east. *Peter Goddard*

Left:
The Southern Region was very rare territory for Class 20s ... until the Hunslet Barclay machines started work for Nomix Chipman! London Bridge commuter platforms host No 20 901 *Nancy* on 14 November 1996 with a Sandite train, with No 20 904 *Janis* out of picture on the rear. No 20 901 was formerly 20 101, and along with all HB's '20s' was sold to DRS and is still in traffic today — with HNRC. *Keith Dungate*

Below:
With No 20 904 *Janis* leading and No 20 901 *Nancy* tailing, an Ashford–Swanley Nomix Chipman weedkilling train passes Tonbridge on 4 May 1993 at the start of the season. The locomotives lost their vacuum brakes on conversion to '20/9s', while Nos 20 902/903/905 were also fitted with extra fuel tanks. *Keith Dungate*

Right:
In 1975/6 BR started withdrawing many diesel-electric locomotives, with massive inroads in the Class 24s as well as the first withdrawals of Class 20s, 26s, 27s, 31s, 40s, 44s. In April 1976 Toton's Pilot Scheme No 20 018 was stored, and condemned on 4 December. After stripping, it was moved to Glasgow St Rollox Works in April 1978 and was scrapped a month later, making this shot on 16 April very rare indeed. No 20 018 displays many of the features of locomotives in the early 1970s — thin black rims on the headcode discs and cabside BR arrows under the numbers and the early type of data panels. It also retains oval buffers. *Brian Daniels*

On death row

Below:
In May 1987 several Class 20s due works attention were placed into store pending possible overhaul. That work was never sanctioned and in November they were condemned. Showing signs of their days in Scotland — Haymarket castle emblems and large numbers — Nos 20 149 and 20 216 rust in peace at the head of a line of Class

Left:
After scrap '20s' were vandalised at Stanton Gate, in early 1992 recently withdrawn machines were stored in sidings at Stapleford & Sandiacre on the approach road to Toton, although even these soon had their windows smashed.
On 10 May the two scrap lines included No 20 196 heading a line of four on the right and No 20 010 in another line. At this time Nos 20 010/028/058/071/082/141/148/ 170/196/197 were all dumped here.
J. Porter / Ivan Stewart collection

Below:
The story of how DRS acquired Class 20s is complicated but started in late 1994 when BNFL bought 15 from RFS and overhauled five. The rest were retained of which two were refurbished along with seven from Racal Telecoms and No 20 042 from Waterman Railways. DRS later acquired seven '20s' from Hunslet Barclay, eight from HNRC, one from EWS and three from preservation groups, meaning it has owned 47 in its lifetime. When other traction was added to the fleet, most notably Class 66s, it sold its remaining stored Class 20s back to HNRC.
No 20 072 stands in front of Nos 20 032, 20 081, 20 215 and 20 088 at the MoD site at Smalmstown, Carlisle on 11 June 2005. All have since been moved to Long Marston for store. *Richard Lillie*

Above:
Between 1976 and 1986 withdrawals of Class 20s were mostly accident-damaged locomotives, but on 20 October 1986 Nos 20 039 and 20 125 were condemned because they were due for overhaul and no sector was willing to pay for the work. By September 1989 there was insufficient space at Toton and stripped '20s' were moved to the sidings at nearby Stanton Gate. Leading the line on 6 March 1990 is No 20 158, with Nos 20 005/054/097/147/086/201/224/193/065/217/179 behind. In late 1990 all moved back to Toton prior to being taken to MC Metals for scrapping. *Paul Biggs*

Below:
Stripped of just about every reusable component, Nos 20 226 and 20 126 stand at MC Metals' yard at Glasgow on 25 March 1992, with four '45s' behind. At this time the site was scrapping locomotives with great speed, and these two machines would only last until June before being disposed of. No 20 226 shows the cab front plate fitted to the last 11 locomotives to allow easier access to the control desks. *Max Fowler*

Left:
MC Metals scrapped 101 Class 20s from 1988 to 1995 when the start of privatisation prevented BR selling assets, eventually forcing the closure of the Scottish breakers' yard. This shot of No 20 143 being cut up in August 1993 may seem typical; however, BR had sold this locomotive for preservation but accidentally despatched it, and it had been scrapped before the error was realised. BR duly released No 20 142 to the Llangollen Railway. *Richard Lillie*

Disposal of assets

Below:
Stripped of major components, the lifeless shell of No 20 167 has been dumped on top of the stack at Vic Berry's scrapyard, Leicester, on 1 October 1988. It rests on half of Class 45/1 No 45 102 and half of '45/0' No 45 009! In the stack are four Class 25s, seven Class 27s and seven other '45s'. No 20 167 shows the mid-1970s trait of applying cabside double arrows below the numbers. 25 Class 20s were scrapped here between 1988 and 1990, and the company also broke up Nos 20 015/076 at Thornaby in 1988. *Craig Shumer*

Above:
Two of Toton's Departmental Sector Class 20s, Nos 20 034 and 20 042 pull into the loop at Fenny Compton with a down ballast trip from Banbury on 24 August 1989. Both machines have Civil Engineers stripes on the cabsides which denoted the area of allocation — in this case LMR — London Midland Region.
No 20 042 has lost its headcode discs at its nose end but not, strangely, at its cab end.
Bryan Hicks

Right:
With Hinckley signalbox in the background and a Bescot-bound freight heading westwards, No 20 147 leads No 20 040 eastbound with a Three Spires–Toton empty MGR on 19 May 1986. *Paul Biggs*

Left:
Grubby in tatty Railfreight livery some eight years after it was overhauled, No 20 132 rests at Skegness on 19 July 1993. This line is still a haven for semaphore signals, but sadly holidaymakers have to travel on DMUs; locomotive-hauled trains are a rarity in 2007. *Robin Ralston*

Below:
Eastfield's Nos 20 083 and 20 175 leave Falkland Yard on 9 August 1982 with a loaded coal. No 20 083 shows all the Scottish hallmarks — large numbers, full set of snowploughs at both ends and discs folded upwards. *John Chalcraft*

A load of ballast

Right:
A Bedford-bound trainload of ballast passes Souldrop, near Sharnbrook with No 20 095 leading No 20 199 on 4 October 1989. This was a typical duty for Class 20s at the time, and the Civil Engineer's Sector had 30 Class 20s allocated to Toton and another four based at Immingham for infrastructure support work. *Keith Dungate*

Below:
Toton's No 20 187 heads through Kilwinning in Ayrshire with an engineers' train on 12 September 1985. At this time it was more common for Toton '20s' to work north of the border — often loaned for weeks at a time. It is fair to say the Scottish Region had fewer qualms about using single Class 20s, and indeed it had several turns for single '20s' which led to pairs not staying together for as long periods as their Midland and Eastern cousins. *J. Porter / Ivan Stewart collection*

Direct and to the point

Right:
Immaculate after overhaul, No 20 310 undergoes static tests at Brush's Loughborough works on 4 June 2005. Brush overhauled the first five '20/3s' for DRS, but the next 10 were by Wabtec at Doncaster. The former No 20 190 looks very different from its BR days — with new light clusters, cantrail headlights, additional fuel tanks and air brakes only. *Richard Lillie*

Below:
DRS has a unique multiple-working system in its fleet, but all classes can work with each other except for its '66s' and a few Class 37s and 57s with blue star multiple working. Hence Class 20/37 pairings are relatively commonplace. The 15.38 Sellafield–Crewe, train 6K73, crosses Arnside Viaduct with No 20 308 leading on 1 August 2005. *Peter Foster*

Above:
In 2005 DRS won four contracts with Network Rail for railhead-treatment trains, which brought the return of top-and-tail Class 20s to infrastructure-control trains. In 2006 10 circuits were awarded to DRS, and the trains in East Anglia and South Yorkshire were Class 20-worked. On 5 October 2006 Nos 20 302 and 20 303 stand at Bradford Interchange. *Mark Allatt*

Top-and-tail treats

Right:
5 September 2005 sees Nos 20 312 and 20 313 top-and-tail train 6Z06, the 09.45 Norwich–Derby, past March. This was the first year that DRS started working railhead-treatment trains and it returned Class 20s to the work for the first time since 1997 when the Hunslet Barclay deal was lost to EWS. *Peter Foster*

Above:
On 8 November 2005 Nos 20 311
and 20 314 work train 1Z63, the
11.50 Wymondham–Stowmarket
railhead-treatment train, seen
crossing the Ouse at Ely Dock.
Peter Foster

Left:
'DRS Anglia on a Mission',
proclaims the headboard — a
common sight on freight trains
these days as depots make their
mark and instil some pride into the
job at the same time. This RHTT is
a little different, as it comprises
two sets — the day train having
picked up the abandoned East
Suffolk RHTT at Wymondham.
This had been caused by a tamper
failure at Stowmarket preventing
the latter's return during the night.
With Nos 20 308/309 leading Nos
20 310/ 311, 1Z63, the 13.12
Wymondham–Stowmarket,
passes Prickwillow (just east of Ely)
on 14 November 2005. *Peter Foster*

Right:
In the summer of 2006 Harry Needle Railroad Company's Nos 20 096 and 20 905 found plenty of use on stock moves for train operators. On 26 April, with No 20 905 leading, the pair pass Sharnbrook on the Midland main line with the colourful three-coach train 5Z30, Derby–Ilford with 'one', GNER and Virgin trailers in tow. *Alisdair Anderson*

Hurry up Harry!

Right:
On 29 June HNRC's Nos 20 096 and 20 905 made a welcome return of a pair of Class 20s to Bescot depot when they arrived to collect No 37 667 to take it to Barrow Hill for overhaul and eventual sale to DRS. Both are fitted with snowploughs and were used by Network Rail on snow clearing duties the previous winter. No 20 096 had a brief spell allocated to Bescot from October 1990 to February 1991 as one of a pool of 12 used for infrastructure trains on the Cross-City Redditch–Lichfield electrification project. No 20 905, however, spent the majority of its BR life as 20 225 in Scotland, from November 1967 to May 1988 when it moved to Immingham and then Toton in July 1988. It was withdrawn in January 1989, sold to Hunslet Barclay and renumbered 20 905. *Andy Williams*

Right:
HNRC's Nos 20 905 and 20 096 arrive at Ely on 26 June 2006 where they will run round train 5N08, the 12.30 Derby Litchurch Lane–Norwich Crown Point stock move, returning 'one' set NC13 after overhaul — it being the last of the refurbished sets for TOC. Both sport snowploughs, fitted to cover a contract for Network Rail on snow-patrol standby duties.
John Day

Ouch!

Above:
Over the years, several '20s' were involved in accidents, some resulting in their condemnation. One early casualty was Tinsley's No 20 033, withdrawn on 23 November 1977 after a collision which caused its cab to droop. To the left is No 20 097 and behind is No 20 081, both of which have minor damage which was repaired. *Brian Daniels*

Below:
Unlike the Class 26 and Class 27s, very few Class 20s suffered fire damage, and only No 20 222 was condemned as a result. The nose-end damage is clear to see in this view at St Rollox on 19 March 1988, a little over three months after it was condemned. Scrapped later that year, in October, the former D8322 had worked for just 20 years. *Brian Daniels*

Kosovo calling

Above:
A most remarkable working by a Class 20 — or indeed any UK locomotive type — occurred in September 1999 when DRS provided three of its recently acquired '20/9s' to work the 'Train for Life' to Kosovo. They worked overland throughout, although were hauled dead in train for much of the way. On the 20th, Czech Republic No 363051 stands next to Nos 20 903, 20 901 and 20 902 at Svitavy. *Bob Sweet*

Right:
Piloted by Bulgarian BZ 45-160, the train with its trio of '20s' pauses at Bov on 24 September 1999, awaiting entry onto the single line to Sofia. The train was organised by Train for Life to take humanitarian aid from Britain. *Bob Sweet*

Above:
Once in Kosovo, part of war-torn Serbia, the '20s' were used by the United Nations Peacekeeping Force in the area for restarting rail services and bringing other loads of humanitarian aid, building materials and supplies from Macedonia. No 20 902 hauls a wagon laden with a French Leclerc tank at Kosovo Polje Yard on 29 September. *Bob Sweet*

Right:
A comparison of European locomotives at Budapest Keleti on 21 September 1999 shows No 20 903 next to OBB No 1014015. This former Eastfield-based No 20 083, which in its career visited all manner of UK destinations while a weedkilling locomotive, can certainly claim to have travelled some miles since it was built in 1961. *Bob Sweet*

Preservation

Right:
Class 20s have proved popular in preservation, both for 'mundane' duties such as infrastructure work, and as an attraction in their own right. Occasionally some railways will go so far as to bring a '20' in as a guest, and in 2006 the South Devon Diesel Traction Group's No 20 118 *Saltburn-by-the-Sea* spent the summer at the Spa Valley Railway. On 6 August it stands at Tunbridge Wells West. *Author*

Below:
The South Devon Railway at Buckfastleigh is home to two preserved '20s', BR blue No 20 110 and Railfreight grey No 20 118 *Saltburn-by-the-Sea*. It has also had guest appearances by four others in recent years, and on 11 June 2006 No 20 118 leads the Class 20 Locomotive Society's No 20 227 off the depot ready to work the first train of the day to Totnes during the line's annual two-day diesel gala. *Author*

Left:
Pioneer No D8000 was saved for the National Railway Museum at York in 1980 when withdrawn on 14 December. At this time BR withdrew several '20s' as traffic fell, but most were reinstated and dual-braked. No 20 050 (as No D8000 had been renumbered in February 1974) spent some time at the NRM unrestored but was repainted green in 1985 at Doncaster. In 1998, using the engine from No 20 078, it returned to traffic and starred at the East Lancashire Railway gala. Since then, visits from the NRM have been rare, but on 4 August 2000 it was at the EWS open weekend at Old Oak Common. *Author*

Right:
After 10 years in traffic in France, CFD ceased using Class 20s in 2002 when the last was laid up. They were offered for sale and a consortium of British preservationists bought all four machines and shipped them back to the UK. On 3 September 2005 the third of the quartet is taken off the ferry at Southampton, CFD No 2004 (ex 20 228). It was operational and is the first, and so far only, one to run back in the UK, based at the Vale of Glamorgan Railway at Barry, South Wales. *Mike Cook*

Right:
Air-brake pipe aside, No D8142 looks much as it did when it was delivered on 21 May 1966 to the Birmingham division (essentially Bescot). It has been based at the Llangollen Railway since 1994 and on 11 October 2003 it has just arrived at Llangollen having piloted No 25 313 on the 15.20 from Carrog. *Author*

Above:
Before Class 20s became relatively commonplace on preserved lines, the North Yorkshire Moors Railway secured the hire of two Thornaby-based Trainload Metals locomotives for its 16 May 1992 diesel gala. Sadly the hoped-for No 20 046, which had not worked a passenger train for 12 years, was stored just beforehand, so it was ex-Toton No 20 214 and No 20 104 that were supplied. They pass Green End heading towards Pickering. *John Hunt*

Left:
One of the best-restored Class 20s has to be No 20 110 at the South Devon Railway, which, with its tablet-catcher recess and black-rimmed discs recreates a Scottish '20' from the mid-1970s to great effect — apart from the fact it is always immaculate rather than work-stained and filthy!
On 12 June 2005 it waits for the signalman to pull off the signal at Staverton so it can call at the station with the 11.00 Totnes Littlehempston-Buckfastleigh.
Author

Below:
DRS Class 20s have always been popular guests for diesel galas, and on 28 March 1999 Nos 20 306 and 20 314 were the star attraction at the Midland Railway, Butterley's event. They lead No 20 001 into Swanwick with a Hammersmith–Riddings train and pass fellow EE machine No 50 007.
Author

In detail

Above:
The picture demonstrates perfectly the differing cabsides on Scottish and English Class 20s. The Scottish machines, illustrated by No 20 127, had deeper cabside windows, recesses for fitting of tablet equipment and a different buffer-beam pipe layout while 'English' No 20 022 has the shallower window design. Reallocations meant both were based at Tinsley on 1 October 1978.
Brian Daniels

Right:
No 20 179 clearly shows the headlight fitted by the Scottish Region, when stabled at Thornton Junction on 21 August 1988. Several ScR Class 20s had these high-intensity headlights fitted in 1986, although strangely No 20 154 had its removed during overhaul in 1987. It wasn't until 1993 that BR decreed that all locomotives should have headlights, by which time Class 20s were few and far between on the main line. *J. Porter / Ivan Stewart collection*

Above:
In the mid-1970s BR took delivery of its first Class 56s and these ousted Class 20s on many coal workings. However it was the arrival of Class 60s in 1990 that saw the Class 20 fleet decimated. At Toton TMD on 22 April 1990 are No 20 004 alongside Romanian-built Class 56 No 56 004 and No 20 053. In October of that year BR withdrew 16 Class 20s in two days — including both these machines, which were, like so many, moved to MC Metals for scrapping. *J. Porter / Ivan Stewart collection*

Left:
The nameplate unveiled on No 20 187 at Pickering on 28 May 1994. When the Railfreight Sector named Class 20s, plates were fitted to the solebar at No 1 end, but Hunslet Barclay and BRT fitted nameplates to the cabsides. When DRS No 20 301 was named *Max Joule 1958-1999* after its late Managing Director, it had just one 'plate, on the cab front. *Author*

Right:
Although many of the fleet were allocated to the Trainload Coal subsector none ever carried its livery — the closest being No 20 088, outshopped in 1988 in two-tone grey Trainload livery but with no subsector markings. Railfreight-grey No 20 010, however, had a small Coal decal applied to its cabside. Missing a '0', and with data panel and railfreight logo, the cabside of the 1957 veteran looks rather shabby and cluttered in this May 1990 picture. *Author*

Sub-class:	20/0	20/3 (BR)	20/3 (DRS)	20/9
TOPS number range:	20 001-228	20 301-308	20 301-315	20 901-906
1957 BR number range:	D8000-8199, D8300-8327			
Built by:	English Electric, Vulcan Foundry, Newton-le-Willows (D8000-19/35-49, 8128-99, 8300-27), and Robert Stephenson & Hawthorn, Darlington (D8020-34/50-127)	Converted: BR Toton	Refurbished: Brush Traction (20 301-305) and Wabtec, Doncaster (20 306-315)	Converted: Hunslet Barclay, Kilmarnock
Introduced:	1957-62 (D8000-127), 1966-68 (D8128-99, 8300-27)	1986	1995 (20 301-305) 1998 (20 306-315)	1989
Wheel arrangement:	Bo-Bo			
Weight:	73 tonnes			
Height:	12ft 7⅜in (3.84m)			
Length:	46ft 9¼in (14.26m)			
Width:	8ft 9in (2.66m)			
Wheelbase:	32ft 6in (9.90m)			
Bogie wheelbase:	8ft 6in (2.59m)			
Bogie pivot centres:	24ft 0in (7.31m)			
Wheel diameter:	3ft 7in (1.09m)			
Minimum curve negotiable:	3.5 chains (70.40m)			
Engine type:	English Electric 8SVT Mk 2			
Engine output:	1,000hp (745kW)			
Power at rail:	770hp (574kW)			
Tractive effort:	42,000lb (187kN)			
Cylinders:	10in bore x 12in stroke			
Maximum speed:	75mph (121km/h)	60mph (97km/h) (20 301-305)	75mph (121km/h) (20 306-315)	60mph (97km/h)
Brake type:	Vacuum, later dual (except 20 003/012/014/ 017/018/024/027/033/ 038/050/074/079/091/109	Dual	Air	Air
Brake force:	35 tonnes			
Route availability:	5			
Main generator type:	EE819-3C			
Auxiliary generator type:	EE911-2B			
Traction motor type:	EE526-5D (8000-50); EE526-8D (D8050-199, 8300-27)	EE526-5D (20 301); EE526-8D (20 302-308)	EE526-5D (20 301); EE526-8D (20 302-315)	EE526-5D (20 904); EE526-8D (20 901-903/ 905/906)
Gear ratio:	63:17	63:17	63:17	63:17

Left:
Underneath the grime, No 20 023 is still in green livery in this 30 September 1978 picture as it leads No 20 010 arriving at Tinsley with train 8E67, the 02.40 freight from Severn Tunnel Junction. The last '20' left in green was No 20 141 — repainted in 1980, some 14 years after the first were repainted blue. No 20 023 still has the opening cock part of its steampipe although the hose section has been removed. Usually it was more common to remove this part as well to leave an open pipe end, which was sometimes plated over.
Danny Preston

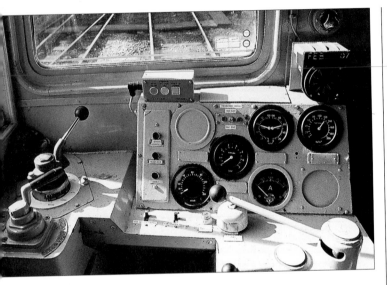

Above:
The driver's desk of No 20 905 shows the bolted-on addition of the train protection warning system display. Two dials have been plated over as the locomotive no longer has train vacuum brakes or slow-speed control. *Author*

Bibliography

The Allocation History of BR Diesels and Electrics, Roger Harris
Profile of the Class 20s, John Vaughan
Class 20s in Colour, Andrew Fell
Class 20 Photofile, Pip Dunn and Martin Loader
Freight Only, Paul Shannon and Michael Rhodes
GEC Traction and its Predecessors, Rodger Bradley
Locomotive Directory, David Strickland
Various issues of *Railways Illustrated*, *Modern Railways*, *Rail*, *Motive Power Monthly magazines*

Acknowledgements

Firstly I would like to thank all the photographers and others who contributed pictures and information for this book. I also thank Chris Stevenson, Steve Smith, Lester French, Darren Stafford and all the members of the Class 20 Locomotive Society and the 'Class 20 Roadshow'. I thank my many friends from the railway publishing world, especially Tony Streeter, Ben Jones, Brian Morrison, Mike Wild and Mel Holley. Finally mention must go to my wife, Victoria who has suffered while the front room was cluttered with pictures, computers and packages all connected with this text and *Railways Illustrated* magazine, and to my family who have supported me over the years, on and off the rails.

Left:
An English Electric 8SVT engine with its EE819-3C main generator still attached removed from a Class 20 at Derby Works in 1987. *Author*